WAR SERVICE ROLL

OF

the Members of The
ROYAL HOUSEHOLDS
and Estates of The
KING and The QUEEN

WAR SERVICE ROLL

of The Members of The
ROYAL HOUSEHOLDS
and Estates of The
KING and The QUEEN

WAR SERVICE ROLL

OF

The Members of The ROYAL HOUSEHOLDS and Estates of The KING and The QUEEN.

(A) KILLED

ADAMS, Arthur, Private.
Under Keeper, Congham Shooting, Sandringham.
Joined, November, 1915.
Norfolk Regiment.
France.
Killed, 19th July, 1916.

ALLEN, Philip, Private.
Gardener, Sandringham.
Joined, 12th October, 1916.
1/4th Norfolks.
Battle of Gaza.
Died of Wounds received at Battle of Gaza.

BALLENY, David, Private.
Porter, Lord Chamberlain's Department.
Joined, March, 1916.
15th Royal Scots.
Killed in Action, 9th April, 1917.

BARRY, William Thomas Henry, Troop Sergeant.
Junior Assistant, Royal Library, Windsor Castle, Lord Chamberlain's Department.
Trooper in S. Mid. Mtd. Brigade, M.M.P.
Corporal in S. Mid. Mtd. Brigade, M.M.P.
Sergeant in Charge in S. Mid. Mtd. Brigade, [M.M.P.
Berkshire Yeomanry.
Gallipoli, Suvla Bay, Hill 60, Egypt, Senussi and Nekhl Expedition, Palestine—1st Battle of Gaza.
Died of Wounds, 17th April, 1917, received same day.

BARTON, B. E., Sergeant.
Royal Mews.
Joined, 7th September, 1914.
R.F.A.
Killed, 23rd September, 1915.

BATTERBEE, Robert Frederick, Private.
Sandringham.
Joined, 12th October, 1916.
3rd Norfolks; 1st Essex.
One engagement.
Killed, 27th January, 1917.

BECK, Frank Reginald, Captain.
Agent to H.M. The King, Sandringham.
1/5th Norfolks.
Gallipoli, August, 1915.
Killed, 12th August, 1915.

BECKETT, Charles, C.S.M.
Gardens, Sandringham.
Joined, 4th August, 1914.
Corporal to Company-Sergeant-Major.
5th Norfolks.
Suvla Bay, Gallipoli; Gaza.
Killed, 2nd Battle of Gaza, 19th April, 1917.

BERKELEY, Thomas Mowbray Martin, Lieut.-Colonel.
His Majesty's Bodyguard of the Hon. Corps of Gentlemen-at-Arms, Lord Chamberlain's Department.
Recruiting Officer, Perth, 6th August, 1914, to January, 1915.
D.A.Q.M.G., 69th Division, January, 1915, to July, 1915, and again at Thetford, July, 1915, to April, 1916.
Camp Commandant, Headquarters, 10th Army Corps, France.
Killed in Action in France, 20th May, 1916.

(A) KILLED

BIGGS, Alfred Ernest, Corporal.
Linen Porter, Lord Chamberlain's Department, Windsor Castle.
Joined, 4th August, 1914.
Corporal, 1915.
Oxford and Bucks Light Infantry.
Loos, Ypres.
Wounded in head, 1915; Shell shock, 1916; Killed, 1917.

BLAKE, Sydney John, Private.
Windsor Royal Gardens.
Joined, 18th February, 1917.
Royal West Surrey.
Military Medal.
Killed at Albert, 24th August, 1918.

BLOGG, Edward Basil, Major.
Clerk, Lord Chamberlain's Office.
Captain, March, 1915; Major, April, 1915.
4th Field Coy., Royal Engineers, 47th London Division (T.F.)
Loos, Hill 70.
D.S.O. at Loos in September, 1915, "for conspicuous gallantry and ability."
Killed in Action, 1916.

BOND, George William, Lance Corporal.
Labourer, Sandringham Farm.
Joined, 29th May, 1915.
Royal Fusiliers.
France.
Killed in France, 28th February, 1918.

BRIDGES, Ernest Edgar, Lance-Corporal.
Under Keeper, Sandringham.
Joined, 1st September, 1914.
Lance-Corporal.
1 5th Norfolks.
1 5th West Riding Regiment.
Somme Battle.
Killed, 17th September, 1916.

BRIDGES, Frederick, Private.
Sandringham.
Joined, 4th August, 1914.
1 5th Norfolks and Essex Regiment.
France.
Killed, 1917.

BUNCE, Charles M.
Assistant Clerk to Master of the Household, Lord Steward's Department.
Joined, 20th April, 1916.
2, 16th Battalion London Regiment (Queen's Westminsters).
Died on Active Service, 12th December, 1917.

BUREAU, Marcel.
2nd Assistant Cook, Lord Steward's Department.
Joined, 8th September, 1914.
168 cme d'infantrie, 31 cme Coy. à Sens.
Killed in France, 12th May, 1915.

BUTLER, William Richard, Private.
Assistant in the Cleaning of the Armour, Windsor Castle, Lord Chamberlain's Department.
Joined, November, 1915.
Berks Yeomanry, Egypt; M.G.C., France.
Egypt and Palestine.
Battles of Nikkli, Hill 60, El Risha, Beilar, Gaza (first and second battles), Beersheba, Al-magar (sword charge), and several engagements in the Judah Hills, near Jerusalem.
Torpedoed, 27th May, 1918, H.M.T. *Leasowe Castle*.
France—Arras, Pevles, Ypres, Passchendaele, Menin Road. Belgium—Courtrai.
Killed in Action, 23rd October, 1918, at Courtrai.

CARPENTER, Albert.
Windsor Royal Gardens.
Joined, 21st November, 1914.
Royal Berks.
France and Belgium.
Killed, 1915.

CHURCH, C., Sergeant.
Footman, Royal Mews.
Joined, 4th September, 1914.
8th Batt., Norfolk Regiment.
Killed, July, 1916.

CLARKE, Alfred, Private.
Windsor Farms.
Royal Berkshire Regiment.
Killed.

(A) KILLED

COOK, James Alfred, Private.
Milk Boy at Sandringham Farm.
Joined, 1st September, 1914.
5th Norfolks.
Gallipoli. Gaza, Palestine.
Killed, 2nd November, 1917.

COOMBER, Herbert, Private.
Gamekeeper, Congham, Sandringham.
Joined, June, 1916.
The Buffs.
France.
Killed in France, 1917.

COX, Joseph H., Private.
Windsor Royal Gardens.
Joined, 12th June, 1916.
8th Batt., Seaforth Highlanders.
Hulloch.
Killed.

CRICHTON, The Viscount, Lieut.-Colonel.
Extra Equerry to the King.
Royal Horse Guards.
Joined, August, 1914.
Killed, October, 1914.

CROFT, Benjamin, Major, T.D.
Accountant, Board of Green Cloth, Lord Steward's Department.
28th Batt., London Regiment (Artists' Rifles).
Substantive Captain, 4th September, 1914; Substantive Major, 19th March, 1918.
B.E.F., 1914.
Killed in Action, 10th November, 1918.

CROSS, Walter, Private.
Gardens, Sandringham.
Joined, 7th April, 1916.
4th East Yorks.
France—Warlencourt.
Killed, Warlencourt, 1916

DANIELS, Harold, Private.
Engineers' Department, Sandringham.
1 5th Norfolks.
Gallipoli. Palestine.
Killed in Palestine, 2nd November, 1917.

DOVE, Robert, Corporal.
Gardens, Sandringham.
Joined, 4th August, 1914.
Private to Corporal.
1 5th Norfolks.
Gallipoli. Suvla Bay.
Killed, Gallipoli, 29th August, 1915.

DUGUID, Robert, Private.
Woods Labourer, Birkhall.
Joined, 3rd March, 1915.
7th Batt., Gordon Highlanders.
Arras, 1917.
Killed at Arras.

DUMONT, Emile, Capitaine.
Pastry Cook, Lord Steward's Department.
France.
51st Regt. Chasseurs Alpins.
Chevalier de la Legion d'Honneur; Croix de Guerre.
Wounded three times.
Died in Elbœuf Hospital, France, 30th August, 1918, from Gas Poisoning.

DUNCAN, Henry, Private.
Roads Labourer, Balmoral.
Joined, 5th August, 1914.
2nd Batt., Gordon Highlanders.
France.
Killed.

EADES, Frederick.
Windsor Royal Gardens.
Joined, December, 1915.
Royal Berks.
France and Belgium.
Killed, 1916.

EDWARDS, William Henry, Private.
Gamekeeper, Windsor. Deputy Rangers.
Joined, 20th November, 1915.
4th Bedfordshire Regiment.
Home Service. Overseas (France).
Killed, 29th April, 1917.

(A) KILLED

EMMERSON, Ernest, Corporal.
Gardens, Sandringham.
Joined, 4th August, 1914.
Private to Corporal.
1 5th Norfolks.
Gallipoli, Suvla Bay.
Killed, 12th August, 1915.

FLYNN, W., Driver.
Royal Mews.
Joined, 4th March, 1915.
Army Service Corps.
Died at Salonica, 1st October, 1918.

GOWER, V. A., Private.
Royal Mews, Windsor.
Joined, 26th December, 1915.
Household Batt. (Life Guards).
Served in France.
Missing.

GREGSON, Robert Cook, Private.
Garden Labourer, Balmoral.
Joined, 1st May, 1917.
3rd Batt., Gordon Highlanders, 1/6th Gordon Highlanders.
Cambrai, 1917.
Killed.

GRIEF, Edward Hugh, Private.
Sandringham.
Joined, 4th August, 1914.
1 5th Norfolks.
Gallipoli, Palestine.
Killed in Palestine, 19th April, 1917.

GROVES, John.
Windsor Royal Gardens.
Joined, December, 1916.
Berks Regiment.
France.
Killed.

HAIGH, George H., Private.
Windsor Royal Gardens.
Joined, 30th November, 1916.
1st and 2nd Batt., Royal Marines.
Passchendaele.
Killed, 26th October, 1917.

HAMILTON, Lord Arthur John, Captain.
Deputy Master of the Household, Lord Steward's Department.
Irish Guards.
France.
Killed in Action, 23rd November, 1914.

HANDLEY, Charles Samuel.
Under Butler, Lord Steward's Department.
Joined, 29th November, 1916.
R.G.A.
Killed in Action, 19th June, 1918.

HARDY, George Henry, Private.
Sandringham.
Joined, 16th June, 1916.
Bedfordshire; Suffolk; 1st Cambridgeshire, attached Royal Engineers.
Battle of Polygon Wood, 26th September, 1917.
Killed, 26th September, 1917.

HOOKS, George L., Private.
Engineers' Department, Sandringham.
Joined, 21st April, 1917.
2nd Middlesex Regiment.
B.E.F., France.
Died as Prisoner of War in Germany, 1918.

HOWELL, James, Private.
Gardens, Sandringham.
Joined, May, 1916.
1 5th Norfolks.
Gaza.
Killed, Gaza, 19th April, 1917.

HUNTER, John, Private.
Woods Labourer, Balmoral.
Joined, 12th August, 1914.
Private to Lance-Corporal.
1 7th Batt., Gordon Highlanders.
Home Service, August, 1914, to April, 1915. France and Belgium, 1st May, 1915, to August, 1916. Second Battle of Festubert, 1915; Somme, 1916.
Died of Wounds, 30th October, 1916.

(A) KILLED

IVALL, Gilbert Edward.
Assistant in Servants' Hall, Lord Steward's Department.
Joined, 5th August, 1914.
1st Batt., Scots Guards.
France.
Killed, 11th November, 1914

JACOBS, Ernest.
Windsor Royal Gardens.
Joined, April, 1915.
Royal Berks.
France.
Killed, September, 1916.

JALLAND, Herbert H., Lieutenant.
Private Secretary's Office.
Joined, 1916.
10th Batt., Black Watch.
Lieutenant.
Salonica. France.
Killed, 1918.

JONES, Henry George.
"Hired Person" in Lord Steward's Department.
Joined, 2nd September, 1914.
3rd Bedfords.
Killed, 21st April, 1915.

JORDAN, William, Private.
Under Keeper, Sandringham.
Joined, 1st September, 1914.
1 5th Norfolks.
Gallipoli and Palestine.
Killed, 19th April, 1917.

KENNEDY, R. W., Corporal.
Footman, Royal Mews.
Joined, 4th September, 1914.
8th Batt., Norfolk Regiment.
Killed, July, 1916.

KERRISON, Frederick, Private.
Gardens, Sandringham.
Joined, 4th August, 1914.
1 5th Norfolks.
Gallipoli, Suvla Bay.
Killed, Gallipoli, 12th August, 1915.

KNIBBS, C., Private.
Royal Mews.
Joined, 2nd January, 1917.
Royal Berkshire Regiment.
Killed, 6th September, 1917.

LINDUPP, Horace, Private.
Windsor Farm.
Joined, September, 1914.
Royal Engineers.
Died of Fever in France.

MacDOUGALL of LUNGA, Stewart, Lieut.-Col.
Gentleman-at Arms.
10th Gordon Highlanders.
Went to France with his regiment on 6th July, 1915, and was killed in action at Vermelles on 21st July, 1915.
Killed in Action.

McDONALD, John, Private.
Garden Labourer, Balmoral.
Joined, 10th September, 1914.
1 7th Gordon Highlanders; 1st Gordon Highlanders.
Festubert, 1915; Somme, 1916; Beaumont Hamel, 1916; Vimy Ridge, 1917; Arras, 1917; Ypres, 1917; Cambrai, 1917; Somme, 1918; La Bassee, 1918; Marne, 1918; Arras, 1918.
Killed, 1918.

McLEOD, T. C., Private.
Footman, Royal Mews.
Joined, 4th September, 1914.
8th Batt., Norfolk Regiment.
Killed, 21st October, 1916.

McNERNEY, Alexander Marr, Privàte.
Assistant Gardener, Balmoral.
Joined, 5th September, 1914.
1 7th Gordon Highlanders.
France.
Died of Wounds.

MERCER-NAIRNE, Lord Charles, Major.
Equerry to the King.
1st Royal Dragoons.
Joined, August, 1914.
Killed, 30th October, 1914.

MUSSETT, Reginald, Private.
Under Keeper, Sandringham.
1/5th Norfolks.
Gallipoli.
Killed, 20th November, 1915.

NEEDS, George William, Lance-Sergeant.
Engineers' Department, Sandringham.
1 5th Norfolks.
Gallipoli.
Killed, 12th August, 1915.

NICHOLSON, Thomas, Trooper.
Road Labourer, Balmoral.
Joined, 5th August, 1914.
1/2nd Scottish Horse; Black Watch.
Gallipoli; Egypt; Salonika; France, 1918.
Died of Wounds.

NURSE, Robert Wallace, Private.
Farm, Sandringham.
Joined, 5th August, 1914.
1 5th Norfolks.
Gallipoli.
Missing, 12th August, 1915.

OLLEY, James, Private.
Under Keeper, Sandringham.
Joined, 25th July, 1916.
Royal West Surrey.
France.
Killed, 1st August, 1917.

PHILLIPS, Frederick Ernest, Private.
Under Keeper, Sandringham.
1 5th Norfolks.
Gallipoli.
Killed, 12th August, 1915.

POXON, Harry James, Gunner.
Windsor Royal Gardens.
Joined, 15th December, 1916.
R.G.A.
Active Service.
Killed.

REED, Horace, Lance-Corporal.
Gardens, Sandringham.
Joined, 2nd June, 1916.
7th Bedfords.
Noyon.
Killed, Noyon, 21st March, 1918.

RINGER, Arthur William, Private.
Sandringham.
Joined, August, 1914.
1/5th Norfolk Regiment; 5th Essex Regiment.
Gallipoli and France.
Killed.

RINGER, Roland Edward, Private.
Sandringham.
Joined, August, 1914.
1/5th Norfolk Regiment.
Gallipoli, Suvla Bay.
Killed.

ROBERTSON, Edward, Private.
Estate Labourer, Balmoral.
Joined, 7th September, 1914.
1/7th Batt., Gordon Highlanders.
Festubert, Somme, Beaumont Hamel, 1916.
Killed, 13th November, 1916.

ROBERTSON, John, K.K., Gunner.
Estate Labourer, Woods, Balmoral.
Joined, 5th August, 1914.
37th Battery, R.F.A.
Mons.
Mentioned, General French's despatches.
Killed, 26th August, 1914.

ROSE, Charles Mchray, Private.
Boy in Balmoral Gardens.
Joined, 8th July, 1916.
3rd Batt., Highland Light Infantry; transferred to 1st Battalion.
Mesopotamia, March, 1917.
Died, Persian Gulf, 26th August, 1917.

(A) KILLED

SKENE, Charles, Driver.
Ploughman, Invergelder; Groom, Birkhall, Balmoral.
Joined, 1st June, 1916.
Royal Engineers.
Salonica.
Died of Fever at Salonica, 15th September, 1918.

SKITTLES, Ernest William, Private.
Windsor Royal Gardens.
Joined, August, 1914.
Berks Regiment.
France.
Died of Wounds, August, 1917.

SMITH, John, Private.
Gardens, Sandringham.
Joined, January, 1915.
Black Watch.
Loos, France.
Killed, Battle of Loos, France, 25th September, 1915.

STEEL, Ernest Edward, Private.
Underkeeper, Sandringham.
Joined, 12th June, 1915.
Royal Fusiliers.
France.
Killed, 3rd May, 1917.

SUTHERLAND, William, Trooper.
Garden Labourer, Abergeldie, Balmoral.
Joined, 5th August, 1914.
1 2nd Scottish Horse.
Gallipoli.
Died of Wounds.

TATE, Isaac, Private.
Windsor Farm.
Royal Berkshire Regiment.
Killed.

THOMPSON, George, Private.
Telephone Operator, Lord Chamberlain's Department.
Joined, 1st January, 1917.
11th Batt., Rifle Brigade; later attached 8th London.
First engagement, 14th August, 1917; last engagement, 30th August, 1918.
Died of Wounds in neck, 1st September, 1918.

THORNDYCRAFT, Edward Charles.
Assistant, Silver Pantry, Lord Steward's Department.
Joined, 3rd September, 1914.
6th Batt., London Regiment.
Killed, 5th November, 1915.

TROUP, William Pope, Private.
Foreman Gardener, Balmoral.
Joined, 16th February, 1916.
3rd Batt., Gordon Highlanders; 1st Batt., Gordon Highlanders.
France—Battle of Guillemont, 18th August, 1916.
Killed, 18th August, 1916.

TWAITE, Arthur, Private.
Labourer, Farm, Sandringham.
Joined, 3rd September, 1914.
8th Norfolks.
France.
Killed in France, 19th July, 1916.

UNDERWOOD, William Arthur.
Assistant, Silver Pantry, Lord Steward's Department.
Joined, 3rd September, 1914.
21st Batt., London Regiment (1st Surrey Rifles).
Killed, 18th May, 1916.

VERTH, William, Private.
Porter, Lord Chamberlain's Department
Joined, 12th November, 1915.
9th Royal Scots, attached 11th Camerons.
France.
Wounded twice—9th April, 1916; 14th August, 1918.
Died of Wounds, 28th August, 1918.

(A) KILLED

WALKER, Robert, Gunner.
Shire Stud Groom, Farm, Sandringham.
Joined, 3rd June, 1916.
R.G.A.
Served in France from 31st December, 1916, to 4th October, 1918, taking part in various battles (names unknown) during this period of service.
Wounded, 22nd September, 1917.
Killed, 4th October, 1918.

WALKER, William.
Sandringham.
9th September, 1914.
1/5th Norfolks.
Gallipoli.
Killed, 12th August, 1915

WEBB, Fred, Private.
Windsor Farm.
Joined, October, 1916.
12th Norfolk Yeomanry Regiment.
Killed.

WILSON, George Henry, Gunner
Upholsterer's Apprentice, Windsor Castle, Lord Chamberlain's Department.
Joined, 26th April, 1915.
R.F.A.
France, October, 1915, attached 36th Irish Division (Ulster). Somme advance, 1916; Messines, 1917.
Killed in Action, 7th April, 1917.

(B) WOUNDED

ADAMS, Frank Henry, Corporal.
Windsor Royal Gardens.
Joined, 14th November, 1914.
From Gunner to Bombardier, March, 1915; Bombardier to Corporal, November, 1917.
R.F.A.
Loos, Ypres, Somme.
Wounded once.

ALCAR, Henry Stafford Howard, Major.
Rouge Dragon Pursuivant of Arms, Lord Chamberlain's Department.
Captain, 21st August, 1915; Major, 18th August, 1917.
Royal Gloucestershire Hussars (Yeomanry).
Egypt, Gallipoli, Sinai, Palestine, Syria, and Turkey in Asia; Chocolate Hill, Gallipoli, 21st August, 1915; Quatea; Romani El Abd; Rafa; first and second battles of Gaza; capture of Beersheba; advance on Jerusalem; raid on Es Salt, east of Jordan; capture of Nazareth, Acre, Damascus and Aleppo.
Despatches, 14th January, 1918; Military Cross, 20th June, 1918.
Wounded twice—21st August, 1915.

ALLEN, John William, Private.
Sandringham.
Joined, April, 1917.
Royal West Kents.
Ypres.
Wounded once.

ALLEN, Robert Henry, Driver.
Sandringham.
Joined, 24th June, 1915.
Royal Engineers.
Battles of Romania, Katier (Egypt), Alrish, Somme, Cambrai (France), Marne.
Wounded once.

ANDREWS, Arthur.
Windsor Royal Gardens.
Joined, 7th January, 1918.
2nd Life Guards and Machine Gun Guards.
France—Albert.
Gassed.

(B) WOUNDED

ANDREWS, Daniel, Private.
Labourer, Game Department, Sandringham.
Joined, 1st September, 1914.
5th Norfolks; 6th Queen's Royal West Surreys.
Battle of the Somme, Vimy Ridge, Messines Ridge, Passchendaele Ridge, March offensive assault on Hindenberg Line.
Taken Prisoner of War.
Wounded twice.

ATHOW, Robert, Corporal.
Gardener, Sandringham.
Joined, November, 1915.
Corporal.
7th Norfolks.
All through the Somme offensive and the Arras Battle and Cambrai and Marby Mailly.
Prisoner of War.
Wounded once.

ATHOW, William, Sergeant.
Gardener, Sandringham.
Joined, 7th August, 1914. Discharged, February, 1919.
Sergeant.
1st Norfolks.
All through the battles which the 1st Norfolks took part in from 1914 to February, 1919.
Wounded twice.

BAILEY, F. A., Bombardier.
Royal Mews.
Joined, 4th August, 1914.
Royal Horse Artillery.
Bombardier.
Ypres, Loos, Somme, Arras, Ancre, Cambrai.
Wounded once.

BARNES, Edward George.
Messenger, Lord Chamberlain's Department.
First, or Grenadier Regiment, Foot Guards.
Ypres.
Wounded once.

BARRY, Ernest, Sergeant Instructor; Corporal Mechanic.
Waterman to H.M., Lord Chamberlain's Department.
Joined, 3rd June, 1915.
Private to Sergeant.
21st London Regiment, Royal Fusiliers (London); R.A.F.
Holding line (trenches), Belgium Frontier.
Physical and Bayonet Instructor (Army); Boat-builder; R.A.F.
Invalided home with neuritis.

BATES, Robert Elijah, Private.
Appleton Farm, Sandringham.
Joined, 21st March, 1916.
1st Bedfords.
Arras, Somme, Ypres.
Wounded three times.

BATTERBEE, George, Sergeant.
Estate Carpenter, Sandringham.
Joined, 4th August, 1914.
Lance-Corporal; Corporal; Sergeant.
1 5th Norfolk Regiment; 1st Gn. Batt., Royal Warwickshire Regiment.
Suvla Bay, 10th August, 1915; Anafarta, 12th August, 1915; continuous service at Gallipoli until evacuated; Egypt, 19th December, 1915, to 31st March, 1916; Sinai Desert from 31st March, 1916, to 31st January, 1917; marched from Egypt to Palestine, February and March, 1917; first battle of Gaza, 25th-26th March, 1917; second battle of Gaza, 19th April, 1917.
Wounded five times.

BEANLANDS, Raymond, Sergeant.
Royal Mews.
Joined, 5th May, 1915.
Royal Army Veterinary Corps, attached to Royal Field Artillery.
Loos, Somme, Arras, Amiens, St. Quentin, Ypres, Meteren, Vimy Ridge, Passchendaele.
Wounded.

(B) WOUNDED

BEDDIE, George, Private.
Garden Labourer, Balmoral.
Joined, 7th March, 1917.
Lovat's Scouts Yeomanry; Machine Gun Corps; Infantry.
Ypres, 1917.
Wounded once.

BELCHER, E. J., Private.
Windsor Royal Gardens.
Joined, 10th December, 1915.
R.A.S.C.; Loyal North Lancs.
Egypt. Palestine—Gaza and Jaffa. France—Albert.
Wounded once.

BENSTEAD, Robert James, Private.
Groom, Stud, Sandringham.
Joined, 1st September, 1914.
Corporal. Reverted, at own request, on joining B.E.F.
Norfolk Regiment; Herts Regiment; Labour Corps.
Battle of Ypres.
Wounded once.

BIGGS, Frederick William, Private.
Sandringham.
Joined, 4th August, 1914.
5th Norfolks, V.T.C.; 3rd Norfolks; 5th Northamptons; Labour Corps in England.
Somme, 1917; Ypres, 1917-18; Messines, 1918.
Wounded three times, slight.

BLAND, Eric, Gunner
Sandringham.
Joined, May, 1916.
Royal Horse Artillery.
France; Germany; Russia.

BOND, William Abraham, Private.
Yardman, Farm, Sandringham.
Joined, 28th May, 1915.
Machine Gun Corps; Royal Fusiliers.
Somme, Arras, Ypres, Cambrai, Bethune.
Wounded twice.

BOUGHEN, Edward L., Private.
Sandringham.
Joined, November, 1915.
37th Royal Fusiliers; transferred Field Labour Company.
Somme.
Wounded once.

BOURDON, René, Private.
Cook, Lord Steward's Department.
Joined, 2nd August, 1914.
41st, 21st, 2nd Regts., French Colonial Infantry.
Lorraine, 1914; Champagne, 1915; L'Oise, 1916; L'Aisne, 1916; La Somme, 1916; La Somme, 1917; Verdun, 1917; St. Mihiel, 1917; Verdun, 1918; Lorraine, 1918; Les Eparges, 1918; Verdun, 1918.
Croix de Guerre; two Stars.
Wounded three times—1914, 1916, 1918.

BOWER, Frank, Sergeant.
Carving School, Sandringham.
Private to Sergeant.
1 5th Norfolks; Royal Flying Corps and Air Force.
Suvla Bay, Gallipoli. Flying in France and Belgium.
Wounded twice.

BRIDGES, Richard, Sergeant.
Under Gamekeeper, Sandringham.
Joined, 1st September, 1914.
Sergeant-Instructor.
1 5th Norfolks; 11th Essex.
Dardanelles—two attacks; France—one attack.
Sergeant-Instructor to H.M. Forces; Physical and Bayonet Training.
Wounded once.

BRIDGES, Wilfred, Acting-Sergeant.
Gamekeeper, Sandringham.
Joined, 14th November, 1911.
1/5th Norfolks.
Suvla Bay, 1915 (12th August); Gaza, 1917 (19th April); Gaza, 1917 (2nd November); Palestine offensive, 1918 (17th September).
Lance-Corporal, March, 1918; Acting-Sergeant, May, 1918.
Wounded twice.

(B) WOUNDED

BROADLEY, Albert Edward, Colour-Sergeant, D.C.M.
Yeoman of the Guard.
Joined, 21st September, 1914.
To Regimental-Sergeant-Major.
Lovat's Scouts Yeomanry, 10th Cameron Highlanders; 7th Squadron Royal Air Force.
Suvla Bay. Lybian Desert. Salonika. France. In trenches at Suvla Bay and Salonika. Driving the Forces of Senussi in Lybian Desert; afterwards with Flying Corps in France.
Wounded once, at Salonika.

BROWN, Charles Harry, Private.
Windsor Royal Gardens.
Joined, 11th December, 1915.
3 1st Berks Yeomanry and 1 4th Royal Berks.
France—Somme and Peronne. Belgium—Flanders, Langemarck, Zonnebeke, Passchendaele Ridge, N.E. of Yypres.
Wounded once.

BROWN, James, Private.
Gardener, Balmoral.
Joined, 24th January, 1916.
16th Batt., Highland Light Infantry.
Somme, 1916; Somme 1917.
Wounded once.

BROWN, Leopold, Private.
Windsor Royal Gardens.
Joined, 11th December, 1915.
6th Reserve Cavalry Regiment, 8th Cavalry Machine Gun Squadron; Berks Yeomanry.
Arras, Cambrai, St. Quentin.
Wounded once.

BROWN, William, Private.
Labourer, Farm, Sandringham.
Joined, 27th September, 1916.
1 6th Norfolk Cyclist Corps; 13th Essex Regiment; 430th Labour Corps.
Battle Front, Passchendaele Ridge, Cambrai.
Wounded once, and gassed.

BUGG, Henry Frederick, Sergeant.
Engineers' Department, Sandringham.
Sergeant.
1 5th Norfolk Regiment; 29th Batt., Middlesex Regiment.
Gallipoli.
I c of R.E. Works' Detachment, Winchester, from 24th May, 1917, to 25th June, 1919.
Mentioned in despatches.
Partially disabled from Enteric Fever.

CARGILL, Charles Smith, Private.
Foreman Gardener, Balmoral.
Joined, 7th September, 1914.
Gordon Highlanders.
Home Service.
France, 1916; Vimy Ridge, 1917.
Wounded once.

CARTER, Maurice, Private.
Windsor Royal Gardens.
Joined, 30th November, 1916.
Royal Marine Light Infantry, 190th Machine Gun Compy., Royal Naval Division.
Arras, Passchendaele Ridge, Cambrai. Mudros.
Gassed.

CHENEY, George Francis, Private.
Windsor Royal Gardens.
Joined, 29th November, 1916.
Royal Marines, 63rd Royal Naval Division.
Arras, Passchendaele, Cambrai.
Gassed.

CHILLEYSTONE, John Henry, Private.
Groom, Sandringham.
Joined, 23rd November, 1915.
King's Own Royal Lancaster.
Salonica, 1916-1917.
Wounded once.

COE, Arthur Richard, Private.
Sandringham, with Mr. Jackson.
Joined, 9th June, 1916.
13th Royal Fusiliers.
Beaumont Hamel, Monchy.
Wounded once.

(B) WOUNDED

COLLIE, George, Private.
Road Labourer, Balmoral.
Joined, 5th August, 1914.
1/2nd Scottish Horse; King Edward Horse; East Surrey Regiment; Trench Mortar Battalion.
Italy. France—Eppes Forest, Bapaume, Hindenburg Line, Caudry, Normal Forest, Lambre, Haltmont.
Wounded once.

COLLINS, Ernest, Sergeant.
Windsor Royal Gardens.
Joined, 19th January, 1915.
Sergeant.
R.F.A.
France and Belgium.
Wounded once.

COLLISON, Frederick, Private.
Sandringham.
Joined, November, 1915.
12th Essex; 25th Training Company; 9th Norfolks; 3rd Norfolks.
Somme, Hulloch, La Bassée.
Wounded once.

COLMAN, Charles, Private.
Farm Labourer, Sandringham.
Joined, 29th February, 1916.
Queen's Royal West Surreys.
Belgium—Vhystrap, Messines Ridge, Ypres.
Wounded once.

COLMAN, Philip, Private.
Sandringham.
Joined, July, 1916.
Royal Engineers.
France.
Wounded once.

COMMON, John, Private.
Porter, Lord Chamberlain's Department.
Joined, 18th November, 1915.
5th Royal Scots; 93rd Field Ambulance; 9th Yorks and Lancs.; 6th Yorks and Lancs.
France.
Wounded twice.

COOK, Thomas George, Captain.
Sandringham.
Joined, February 18th, 1915.
Norfolk Regiment; Irish Batt., King's Liverpool Regiment; Royal Fusiliers.
2nd Lieutenant to Captain.
Ypres.
Wounded once.

COX, Percy, Private.
Farm Labourer, Sandringham.
Joined, 20th June, 1916.
1st Norfolks.
France—Hoppy Wood, Arras, Ypres.
Wounded once.

CRISP, Mark, Private.
Gamekeeper, Sandringham.
Joined, 30th November, 1915.
3 4th Norfolks.
France.
Wounded three times.

CROSS, Frederick William, Private.
Sandringham.
Joined, 4th August, 1914.
1 5th Norfolks.
Battle of Suvla Bay; Second Battle of Gaza.
Wounded once. Prisoner.

CROWE, Robert John, Corporal.
Carter (Nurseries), Farm, Sandringham.
Joined, 4th August, 1914.
1 5th Norfolks.
Gallipoli Peninsula. Suez Canal. Egypt, Palestine. Suvla Bay, 12th August, 1915.
Wounded once.

(B) WOUNDED

DAVIS, E., Lieutenant.
Steward's Room Assistant, Lord Steward's Department.
Joined, 1st September, 1914.
Corporal (Queen's Westminster Rifles), March, 1916; 2nd Lieutenant, 4th Durham Light Infantry, 25th October, 1916; Lieutenant, 4th Durham Light Infantry, 25th April, 1918.
16th County of London Regiment (Queen's Westminster Rifles); 4th Batt. (S.R.), Durham Light Infantry.
Trench warfare, 25th January, 1915, to 23rd April, 1916; Armentières to Ypres, including Battle of Hooge, 9th August, 1915 (6th Division); gas attack made by Germans at Ypres, 19th December, 1915; trench warfare from 5th January, 1917, to 23rd May, 1917, including raid by enemy 13th May, 1917, heavily repulsed; Italy—Piave and Asiago Plateau, 14th January, 1918, to 15th April, 1918, heavy patrol fighting.
M.C., 13th May, 1917.
Wounded, Italy, 15th April, 1918, right foot. Amputation right leg below knee, 3rd May, 1918.

DAW, Percy, Private.
Under Gamekeeper, Sandringham.
1st Norfolk Regiment.
France.
Wounded once.

DAW, Sidney, Gunner.
Under Gamekeeper, Sandringham.
Joined, 6th June, 1916.
Royal Garrison Artillery.
Somme, Ypres, Bethune, Arras.
Wounded once.

DAW, William, Private.
Gardens, Sandringham.
Joined, 4th August, 1914.
1 5th Norfolks; 1 6th Duke of Wellington's, 49th Division.
Somme and Western Front from August, 1916.
Territorial.
Wounded twice and gassed.

DELAHUNT, James, Corporal.
Royal Mews.
Joined, 7th September, 1914.
Royal Field Artillery.
Corporal.
Loos, Somme, Vimy, Messines, Newport, Cambrai. Italy.
Wounded once.

DIXON, Clifford, Private.
Gardens, Sandringham.
Joined, 3rd December, 1915.
Lance-Corporal.
Essex Regiment.
Somme, 1916; Passchendaele, 1917.
Wounded twice.

DOEL, Joseph Albert, Private.
Assistant Gamekeeper, Windsor. Deputy Rangers.
Joined, 8th April, 1916.
2nd Royal Berks, 5th Army Corps, Flying Column.
Somme, Ypres, Messines, Plug Street, La Bassée.
Prisoner of War.
Wounded once.

DUNGER, Robert John, Pioneer.
Sandringham.
Joined, 26th May, 1915.
R.E.
Somme, Arras, Passchendaele, Ypres to Germany.
Gassed, Wounded.

DYE, George Walter, Sergeant.
Farm Labourer, Sandringham.
Joined, 10th June, 1915.
Lance-Corporal, Corporal, Sergeant.
Royal Fusiliers; Royal West Kents; Labour Corps.
Battle of Messines.
Bombing N.C.O.
Gassed on 26th July, 1917.

EARWAKER, Frederick George, Sergeant.
Royal Mews.
Joined, 5th August, 1914.
Royal Horse Artillery.
Bombardier to Sergeant.
Ypres, Loos, Neuve Chapelle, Cambrai.
Wounded once.

(B) WOUNDED

ELLIS, Gerald M. A., Major.
Gentleman Usher, Lord Chamberlain's Department.
Major, Second in Command, 2nd Batt., Rifle Brigade, 1917. In command of Battalion when wounded, thereby losing promotion to Lieut.-Colonel.
Rifle Brigade.
Flanders and France—Ypres, 1915 (Second Battle); Somme, 1917; attack and capture, Gonnetiere in Gouzeaucourt.
Attached General Staff, War Office, 1916, and again 1918 until end of year.
Wounded twice (severely).

EYRES, William John, Private.
Windsor Royal Gardens.
Joined, 29th November, 1916.
Royal Marines, 63rd Royal Naval Division.
Arras, Passchendaele, Cambrai.
Wounded twice.

FISHER, Edwin Charles, Corporal.
Royal Mews.
Joined, 5th August, 1914.
Royal Horse Artillery.
Corporal.
1914-18. All actions with Royal Horse Artillery, 7th Brigade, 1st Cavalry Division.
Gassed.

FLEGG, Ernest Willie, Corporal.
Woods, Sandringham.
Joined, 8th December, 1915.
Corporal.
8th East Surrey.
Somme, Arras, Ypres. St. Quentin.
Wounded once.

FOSTER, William, Private.
Windsor Farms.
Joined, December, 1914.
Royal Berks Regiment.
Wounded twice.

FRASER, John, Company-Sergeant-Major.
Cabinet Maker, Lord Chamberlain's Department.
Joined, 2nd July, 1915.
Company-Sergeant-Major.
9th Batt., Royal Scots.
Western Front. Somme, 1916; Arras, 1917; Cambrai, 1918; Soissons, 1918.
D.C.M., Medal Militaire (French), Croix de Guerre (French).
Wounded once.

FRENCH, Charles George, Corporal.
Gamekeeper, Sandringham.
Joined, 15th November, 1915.
Corporal.
Royal Fusiliers.
Battles of the Somme, Arras, Cambrai, Retreat from Cambrai, the Big Advance, march to the Rhine.
Once gassed.

GODFREY, David, Private.
Wolferton Farm, Sandringham.
5th Batt., Norfolk Regiment; 2nd Batt., City of London (Royal Fusiliers).
France.
Wounded once.

GOODSHIP, Raymond Thomas, Private.
Under Gamekeeper, Sandringham.
Joined, 1st September, 1914.
1 5th Norfolks.
Gallipoli, 1915; Egypt, 1916; France, 1918.
Wounded once.

GOODSHIP, Sidney William, Sergeant.
Under Gamekeeper, Sandringham.
Joined, 16th November, 1911.
Sergeant.
1 5th Norfolks.
Gallipoli, 1915; Egypt, 1916.
Wounded three times.

GOODSHIP, William, Private.
Carving School, Sandringham.
Joined, 2nd November, 1914.
1 5th Norfolks; Northumberland Fusiliers; 2nd Duke of Wellirgton's (West Riding Regiment).
France and Belgium.
Wounded twice.

(B) WOUNDED

GRAY, Owen Sidney, Private.
Royal Mews.
26th August, 1914.
Northamptonshire Regiment, 1st and 5th.
Ypres, Armentières, Hulloch, Loos, Givenchy, Somme, Arras, Monchy-le-Preux, Cambrai, Laventie, Somme.
Wounded once.

GRAY, Robert William, Driver.
Royal Mews.
Joined, 4th August, 1914.
Royal Field Artillery.
Mons. Mesopotamia, Kut-el-Amara. Passchendaele, Menin Road.
Wounded once.

GREEN, Fred.
Windsor Royal Gardens.
Joined, 27th October, 1914.
Royal Field Artillery.
Somme and Peronne.
Wounded once.

GRIMES, Arthur, Lance-Corporal.
Sandringham.
Joined, 4th August, 1914 (8 years in Territorials before the War).
5th Norfolks; 3rd Northants; 7th Norfolks.
Gallipoli; Egypt; Battle of Anafarta; Battles in France, Arras, Cambrai, Albert, Somme.
Wounded once.

GRIMES, Robert, Private.
Sandringham.
Joined, 15th September, 1914.
1 5th Batt., Norfolk Regiment.
Gallipoli. Battles taken part in: Anafarta, Egypt and Palestine, 1st and 2nd Battles of Gaza and El Terek.
Wounded once.

GRINDLEY, Frederick, Lance-Corporal.
Windsor Royal Gardens.
Joined, 12th June, 1915.
Lance-Corporal.
Seaforth Highlanders.
Hulloch, Somme, Arras, Monchy, Ypres, Zillibeke, Meteren.
Wounded three times.

HALL, Thomas James, Private.
Royal Mews.
Joined, 15th September, 1914.
Berks Yeomanry; Imperial Camel Corps; Worcester Yeomanry.
Gallipoli, Suvla Bay, Hill 70. Palestine Front. Beersheba. Jordan Valley.
Wounded once.

HAMMOND, Robert John, Lance-Corporal.
Gamekeeper's Labourer, Castle Rising, Sandringham.
Joined, 1st June, 1915.
Lance-Corporal.
Royal Fusiliers.
Somme, Ypres, Cambrai.
Wounded once. Gassed once.

HAMMOND, Thomas W., Private.
Woods, Sandringham.
Joined, 25th January, 1915.
3rd Norfolks; transferred to 7th Border.
Ypres, Hill 60, Armentières, Laventie, St. Eloi, Zillebeche, Sanatorium Wood, Ploogstraet Wood, Neuve Chapelle, Festubert.
Wounded once.

HENDERSON, Charles, Private.
Assistant Gardener, Balmoral.
Joined, 11th February, 1916.
Seaforth Highlanders.
Salonika, 1916; Strume Front, 1918; Mount Kemmel, 1918; Meteron, 1918; Ypres, 1918.
Wounded twice—1917, 1918.

HICKS, Ernest Walter, Private.
Windsor Royal Gardens.
Joined, 8th December, 1915.
Royal Berks Regiment.
Arras, Cambrai, Malard Wood, Trones Wood.
Wounded three times.

HODGES, Walter, Sergeant.
Groom, Stud, Sandringham.
Joined, 3rd March, 1916.
Lance-Corporal, Corporal, Sergeant.
9th Batt., Norfolk Regiment.
Somme, Hulloch, Cambrai, Queant, Neuve Eglise, Brancourt, Basuel, Ginchy, Lens, Marcoing, Kemmel, Holnon Wood, Bohain.
Wounded once.

(B) WOUNDED

HOLMES, William Thomas, Regimental-Sergeant-Major.
Privy Purse Office.
King's Royal Rifles.
Regimental-Sergeant-Major.
Ypres, Somme, Arras.
Military Cross.
Wounded twice.

HOUCHEN, George James, Lance-Corporal.
Engineers' Department, Sandringham.
Joined, 4th August, 1914.
Lance-Corporal.
1 5th Norfolks.
Gallipoli, 12th August, 1915; Gaza, 19th April, 1917; Tiveh, 15th December, 1917; Kaffiar-Khsam, 19th September, 1918.
Wounded twice.

HOUSE, Frank, Private.
Inventory Clerk, Lord Chamberlain's Department.
Joined, 24th April, 1915.
2nd London Regiment (Royal Fusiliers).
France—Arras, 1917.
Transferred to Labour Corps, March, 1918.
Shell Shock.

HOWELL, David, Private.
Sandringham.
Joined, 4th August, 1914.
Norfolk Regiment.
Gallipoli; Egypt; Palestine, Suvla Bay, Gaza, 1917.
Wounded once.

HUDSON, William, Lance-Corporal.
Sandringham.
Joined, 4th August, 1914.
Norfolk, Northumberland Fusiliers, and Duke of Wellington's W.R.R.
Somme, Ypres, Amiens, Bapaume, Havrincourt and Epehy, Cambrai and Hindenburg Line, Battle of the Selle.
Wounded three times.

HUGHS, William.
Windsor Royal Gardens.
Joined, 16th April, 1915.
Warwickshire Regiment.
France.
Wounded twice. Gassed once.

JACKSON, Edward Charles, Sergeant.
State Room Porter, Lord Chamberlain's Department.
Joined, 29th December, 1914.
Lance-Corporal, March, 1915; Corporal, July, 1916; Sergeant, September, 1916.
1 23rd London Regiment; 1/17th London Regiment.
France—Festubert, Givenchy, Vimy Ridge, Somme (September), 1916, Lille. Belgium—Tournai.
Wounded three times—Givenchy, May, 1915; Vimy Ridge, May, 1916; Somme, October, 1916.

JAKEMAN, William, Sergeant.
Gardens, Sandringham.
Joined, 4th August, 1914; Discharged, 17th December, 1915; Re-joined, 16th August, 1916.
Full Sergeant.
1/5th Norfolks (Territorials); 4th Reserve Batt., Norfolks.
Suvla Bay landing, Gallipoli, and after advance.
Wounded three times.

KEMP, J., Sergeant.
Royal Mews.
Joined, 27th August, 1914.
Grenadier Guards.
Private to Sergeant.
Festubert, Aublens, Givenchy, Loos, Ypres, Hulloch, Somme.
Wounded twice.

KYDD, John, Lance-Corporal.
Assistant Gardener, Balmoral.
Joined, 5th September, 1914.
7th Batt., Gordon Highlanders, Foot Police.
Lance-Corporal.
Festubert, 1915; Arras, 1916; Vimy Ridge, 1916; High Wood, 1916; Death Valley, 1916.
Wounded once.

LANE, Henry Edward, Corporal.
Gardens, Appleton, Sandringham.
Joined, 1st June, 1915.
Lance-Corporal, Corporal.
Royal Fusiliers.
France and Belgium. Arras, 1916; Somme, 1916; Messines, 1917.
Wounded twice.

(B) WOUNDED

LANFEAR, J., Driver.
Windsor Royal Gardens.
Joined, 22nd March, 1915.
Royal Army Service Corps.
Dardanelles. Egypt. Palestine. Gaza. France.
Wounded once.

LAWRENCE, George, Sergeant-Drummer, D.C.M.
Yeoman of the Guard.
Joined, 23rd November, 1914.
To Regimental-Sergeant-Major.
8th Batt., Gordon Highlanders.
France—Loos, Hill 60.
Wounded once (slightly).

LEE, Arthur, Private.
Under Keeper, Sandringham.
Joined, 9th December, 1915.
7th Suffolk Regiment, 35th Brigade; 12th Division Labour Corps.
Western Front—Somme, Infantry Hill, Arras, Monchy-le-Preux, Cambrai.
Wounded once.

LINFORD, Clarence, Lance-Corporal.
Royal Mews.
Joined, August, 1914.
1st Suffolk Regiment.
Private to Lance-Corporal.
Western Front—second Battle of Ypres.
Wounded once.
Prisoner of War in Germany, three years and eight months.

LINFORD, Herbert, Company-Quarter-Master-Sergeant and Acting-Commander-Company-Major.
Gamekeeper, Sandringham.
Company-Quarter-Master-Sergeant, Acting-Company-Sergeant-Major.
5th Batt., Norfolk Regiment; 14th Queen's (Royal West Surreys); Labour Corps, 96th Compy.
Suvla Bay, Gallipoli. Salonica.
Mentioned in Despatches.
Wounded once.

MACKINTOSH, Victor, Private.
Woods Labourer, Balmoral
Joined, 6th December, 1915.
3 7th Gordon Highlanders; 1/7th Gordon Highlanders.
Battle of the Somme, Beaumont Hamel.
Discharged.
Wounded once.

MACLEAN, Simon, Private.
Valet.
Joined, 11th March, 1915.
14th London Regiment (London Scottish).
France—26th February, 1916, to 1st July, 1916—Gommecourt Wood.
Wounded.

MAINE, Henry Cecil Sumner, Lieutenant.
Private Secretary's Office.
Joined, February, 1916.
Grenadier Guards.
Lieutenant.
Somme.
Wounded once.

MAITLAND, Viscount F. C., Colonel.
Hon. Corps of Gentlemen-at-Arms.
23rd Batt., Royal Fusiliers; 3rd (H.S.) Garr. Batt., Northumberland Fusiliers.
Flanders, August, 1915 (four days); France, November, 1915, to February, 1916.
Wounded once.

MARRINGTON, William, Private.
Sandringham.
Joined, May, 1916.
East Surrey Regiment, Queen's Royal West Surrey, Labour Corp, Suffolk Regiment.
Beaucourt.
Wounded once.

MARSTERS, Sidney, Private.
Under Keeper, Sandringham.
Joined, 1st September, 1914.
Sergeant.
1 5th Norfolks.
Suvla Bay. Three Battles of Gaza. Stone Hill.
Wounded twice.

(B) WOUNDED

MAY, A., Private.
Windsor Royal Gardens.
Joined, 11th March, 1915.
Loyal North Lancs.
Passchendaele.
Gassed.

McCARTNEY, James, Private.
Gardens, Sandringham.
Joined, 18th February, 1916.
Royal West Surreys; Machine Gun Corps.
France, 1st March, 1917, to 8th May, 1917.
Wounded once.

McCONNOCHIE, William, Private.
Windsor Royal Gardens.
Joined, 12th June, 1915.
Seaforth Highlanders; Gordon Highlanders (9th Pioneers).
Loos, Somme, Arras, Soissons, Grand Offensive, 1918.
Wounded once.

McGREGOR, James, Private.
Wood Labourer, Balmoral.
Joined, 10th September, 1914.
1 7th Gordon Highlanders.
Festubert, 1915; Somme, 1916; Beaumont Hamel, 1916; Vimy Ridge, 1917; Arras, 1917; Ypres, 1917; Cambrai, 1917; Somme, 1918; La Bassee, 1918; Marne, 1918; Arras, 1918; Cambrai, 1918.
Wounded once.

McILVEEN, Frederick Thomas, Gunner.
Royal Mews.
Joined, 28th November, 1916.
Royal Horse Artillery.
Bombardier.
France and Germany.
Wounded once.

MERRYMAN, Edward, Private.
Windsor Royal Gardens.
Joined, 24th November, 1914.
Oxford and Bucks Light Infantry.
Loos; Belgium.
Wounded once.
Prisoner of War.

MITCHELL, Albert Edward, Lance-Corporal.
Sandringham.
Joined, 4th August, 1914.
1 5th Norfolks.
Gallipoli. Egypt.
Wounded once.

MITCHELL, Frederick Charles, Private.
Royal Mews.
Joined, 1st November, 1915.
Civil Service Rifles (15th London).
Salonika; Egypt; Palestine. Western Front.
Wounded once.

MURKING, W., Gunner.
Royal Mews.
Joined, 10th August, 1914.
235th Brigade R.F.A., 47th Division.
Festubert, Loos, Vimy, High Wood, Eaucourt L'Abbaye, Messines, Menin Road, Cambrai, Bapaume, Albert, Combles, Lille.
Wounded once.

NEWTON, John Robert, Private.
Coal Porter, Lord Steward's Department.
1st Batt., Grenadier Guards.
Neuve Chapelle, Festubert, Loos.
Wounded once, 1915.

NICHOLSON, John, Private.
Woods Labourer, Balmoral.
Joined, 5th August, 1914.
7th Gordon Highlanders; Labour Corps.
Beaumont Hamel.
Wounded once.

NICHOLSON, John T., Corporal.
Royal Mews.
Joined, 7th September, 1914.
Royal Horse Guards.
Corporal, December, 1915.
Ypres (second battle), Somme, Arras, Cambrai.
Wounded twice.

NORWAK, Charles Frederick, Lieutenant.
Confectioner, Lord Steward's Department.
Joined, November, 1915.
2nd Lieutenant, April, 1917; Lieutenant.
7th Batt., Norfolk Regiment.
Arras, 1917; Monchy-le-Preux, 1917.
Gas Poisoning and Shell Shock.

(B) WOUNDED

NURSE, Arthur Albert, Private.
Sandringham Farm.
1 5th Norfolks (T.F.).
Mediterranean Expeditionary Force, 7th February, 1916, to 25th June, 1917.
Gaza Battle and Belmont Hill.
Buried. Shell Shock.

OSBORNE, R. J. P., Private.
Windsor Royal Gardens.
Joined, 8th January, 1918.
2nd Life Guards; Machine Gun Guards.
Somme, St. Quintin. Russia.
Gassed.

OSGOOD, James, Sergeant-Major.
Windsor Royal Gardens.
Joined, 5th August, 1914.
Sergeant-Major.
Berkshire Regiment.
France and Belgium.
Military Medal.
Wounded twice.

PAYNE, A., Lance-Corporal.
Windsor Royal Gardens.
Joined, 30th May, 1916.
9th King's Own Yorkshire Light Infantry.
Ypres.
Wounded once.

PAYNE, Joseph, Sergeant-Major, M.C., D.C.M.
Yeoman of the Guard.
Joined, 16th April, 1915.
Lieutenant, 28th December, 1915; Captain, 20th May, 1916; Acting-Major, General List, October, 1917; Lieut.-Colonel, 11th April, 1918.
11th Batt., South Lancs. Regiment.
France, 1915. Mailly, Mailly sector, November-December, 1915; Froissy and Cappy during "Frise" incident, February, 1916; Somme, 1st to 31st July, 1916; Nerville St. Vaast, August, 1916; Givenchy, September, 1916; Somme, October-November, 1916; Wyschette sector, September-October, 1917; Ypres sector, February-March, 1918; German offensive, Neuve Eglise, Dranoutre, and Kimmel Hill, April, 1918; Walroy and Sailly le Sec, July, 1918; Commandant Reinforcement Training Camp No. 2, to 25th May, 1919.
M.C. and Bar.
Gassed on Somme.

PEEL, Vyvian Neville, Lieutenant.
Resident Clerk, Lord Chamberlain's Office.
Joined, 10th August, 1914.
2nd Lieutenant, Lieutenant.
Inns of Court O.T.C.; Argyll and Sutherland Highlanders; Royal Flying Corps.
France, 1915, with Argyll and Sutherland Highlanders and No. 3 Squadron, R.F.C.; France, 1916, 2nd Batt., Argyll and Sutherland Highlanders, during part of the Somme Battle; employed in 1917 in Mineral Resources Department, Ministry of Munitions, and in 1918 in the Intelligence Department of the Admiralty.
Shell Shock.

RALPH, Alfred, Bombardier.
Windsor Royal Gardens.
Joined, 2nd February, 1915.
From Gunner to Bombardier.
Royal Field Artillery.
France, Somme. Belgium, Ypres. Italy. Nieuport.
Wounded once.

RANSOME, Frank Langley, Lance-Corporal
Woods, Sandringham.
Joined, 2nd June, 1916.
Lance-Corporal.
7th Bedfords and 2nd Bedfords.
France, 1916 to 1918. Somme, Yypres, Passchendaele Ridge, Cambrai, St. Quentin, Arras, Albert, Thiepval.
Wounded twice—1917 and 1918. Gassed in 1917.

RENN, Henry Thomas, Corporal.
Coal Porter, Lord Steward's Department.
Joined, 4th September, 1914.
Appointed Corporal, 24th December, 1916.
6th City of London Rifles.
Loos, Somme, Messines, The Bluff (Ypres).
Wounded twice.

RICHES, George William, Private.
Woods, Sandringham.
Joined, 11th December, 1915.
3rd Norfolks; transferred to 1 5th Norfolks.
Egyptian Expeditionary Force.
Gaza, 26th March, 1917; Gaza, 19th April, 1917; Gaza, 2nd November, 1917; Syria, 18th September, 1918.
Wounded once.

(B) WOUNDED

RICHES, William James, Lance-Corporal.
Sandringham.
Joined, December, 1917.
Northampton Regiment; Bedfordshire Regiment; Beds and Herts Regiment.
Lance-Corporal.
Battles of St. Quentin, Arras, and Sambre-Oise Canal.
Wounded. Slightly gassed.

ROBERTSON, Ean Stewart, Lance-Corporal.
Estate Labourer, Birkhall, Balmoral.
Joined, 19th November, 1914.
7th Gordons, 1st Gordons, 16th Batt., Tank Corps.
Lance-Corporal.
Serre, 1916; Arras, 1917; Monchy, 1917; Ypres, 1917; St. Quentin and Cambrai, 1918.
Wounded once.

ROGERS, Joseph William, Corporal.
State Room Porter, Lord Chamberlain's Department.
Joined, 5th April, 1915.
Corporal, at Gallipoli.
1 11th London Regiment; 813rd A.E. Coy. Labour Corps.
Gallipoli. Suez Canal zone. Egypt. Palestine.
Wounded once, at Gaza.

ROWSELL, Herbert, Driver.
Royal Mews.
Joined, 26th April, 1915.
Army Service Corps and Royal Field Artillery.
Palestine.
Wounded twice.

SAINSBURY, Henry.
Windsor Royal Gardens.
Joined, 7th December, 1916.
Royal Berks; Machine Gun Regiment.
France and Belgium.
Gassed.

SEARS, John, Private.
Windsor Royal Gardens.
Joined, 6th March, 1917.
Royal Marines.
Passchendaele. Belgium.
Wounded once.

SEYMOUR, Mark, Corporal.
Joiner, Lord Chamberlain's Department.
Joined, 29th December, 1914.
84th Field Compy., R.E.
Corporal.
Somme offensives, 1916.
Wounded once.

SEYMOUR, R. H., Major.
Equerry.
King's Royal Rifle Corps.
Major.
Aisne, Ypres.
Wounded once.

SHAW, Albert, Rifleman.
Coal Porter, Buckingham Palace, Lord Steward's Department.
Joined, 1st June, 1915.
18th London Irish.
Somme.
Wounded once.

SIMMONS, Abel, 2nd Corporal.
Farm, Sandringham.
Lance-Corporal, 2nd Corporal.
1/5th Norfolks; Royal Engineers.
Somme, Arras, Ypres, Hargicourt Hill, St. Quentin, Somme, Armentières.
Military Medal.
Wounded once. Gassed. Buried twice.

SLADE, Walter, Private.
Royal Mews.
Joined, 3rd May, 1915.
6th East Surreys and Royal Fusiliers.
Somme, Arras, Passchendaele Ridge, Cambrai.
Accident.

SOTHEBY, Herbert George, Lieut.-Colonel, M.V.O.
Privy Purse Office.
Argyll and Sutherland Highlanders.
Captain, 1902; Major, 1916; Lieut.-Colonel, 1916.
Somme, Ypres, Arras, Passchendaele, Amiens, Bapaume, Epéhy, Cambrai, St. Quentin, Selle River, Mauberge.
D.S.O., Croix de Guerre (Gold Star) French, three times mentioned in Despatches.
Wounded once.

(B) WOUNDED

SPARROW, Thomas, Private.
Sandringham.
Joined, February, 1916.
Queen's Royal West Surrey Regiment and Machine Gun Corps.
Somme, Monchy.
Wounded twice.

STINTON, Fred, Sapper.
Assistant French Polisher, Windsor Castle, Lord Chamberlain's Department.
Joined, 15th February, 1915.
Lance-Corporal.
Royal Engineers (T.F.).
Western Front, June, 1915, to October, 1916. Loos, September, 1915; Somme, 1916.
Croix de Guerre.
Wounded twice.

STOCKLEY, Henry Hudson Fraser, Major.
Clerk in the Lord Chamberlain's Department.
Major (Temporary), February, 1916; Major (Substantive), 7th October, 1916.
Portsmouth Batt., Royal Marine Light Infantry.
With Royal Marine Brigade at Ostend, August, 1914; operations near Lille and Tournai, and Defence of Antwerp, September-October, 1914; with Royal Marine Brigade at Port Said, Egypt, March, 1915; landed at Gaha Tepe, Gallipoli Peninsula, 28th April, 1915.
Mentioned in Despatches.
Wounded, 3rd May, 1915 (Gallipoli). Right leg amputated, 12th May, 1915, at Alexandria.

STOKES, John, Sergeant.
Sandringham.
Joined, 4th August, 1914.
1 5th Batt., Norfolk Regiment.
Corporal, Acting-Sergeant.
Gallipoli. Palestine. Gaza. Egypt.
Wounded once.

THOMPSON, F., Lance-Corporal.
Royal Mews.
Joined, 9th September, 1914.
Queen's Own Oxford Hussars and 3rd County of London Yeomanry.
Lance-Corporal.
France. Egypt. Palestine.
Wounded once.

TOSELAND, Herbert George, Lieutenant.
Royal Library, Windsor Castle, Lord Chamberlain's Department.
Joined, 10th September, 1914.
2 2nd London Field Ambulance, Royal Army Medical Corps (T.); 19th Batt., London Regiment.
Overseas service six months.
Ypres, September, 1917.
2nd Lieutenant, 30th May, 1917. Lieutenant, 30th November, 1918.
Wounded once.

TRUNDLE, Henry Ernest, Private.
Sandringham.
Joined, 15th January, 1915.
1st Norfolks.
Somme three times), Vimy Ridge (twice), Arras (twice).
Wounded once.

TURLEY, Frederick Percy, Corporal.
Sandringham.
Joined, 4th August, 1914.
1 5th Norfolks.
Corporal.
Gallipoli. Egypt. Palestine. Syria. Suvla. Gaza.
Wounded once.

TWYMAN, Arthur John, Sergeant.
Assistant Cellarman, Lord Steward's Department
Joined, 5th September, 1914.
Lance-Corporal, October, 1914; Corporal, June, 1915; Sergeant, February, 1916.
2 21st London Regiment; also 21st (Reserve) London Regiment.
Proceeded to join the B.E.F. in May, 1916, with 2 21st London Regiment, 60th Division, and relieved the 51st Highland Division at Roclincourt, on the Arras salient. On being invalided home, joined Reserve Battalion, and was appointed Battalion Messing Sergeant, and later Officers' Mess Sergeant.
Shell Shock (once .

(B) WOUNDED

TYRWHITT, Hon. Leonard, Canon, M.A., M.V.O.
Chaplain - in - Ordinary, Lord Chamberlain's Department.
Joined, 12th October, 1914.
March, 1915, from 4th Class to 3rd Class; January, 1918, from 3rd Class to 2nd Class.
8th Division, 23rd Infantry Brigade (Brigade Chaplain). 57th Division, 1916-18. Senior Chaplain, 10th Corps Headquarters, 1918-19.
Neuve Chapelle, Armentières, Langemarck, Pilkem Ridge, Bosinghe, St. Pol, Arras, Doulens. Lessines, Andennes, Bonn. France. Belgium. Germany.
Mentioned in Despatches.
Wounded once.

WALKER, Thomas, Private.
Gamekeeper, Sandringham.
Joined, 9th December, 1915.
Regimental Police.
8th Batt., Northants; 9th Batt., King's Own Royal Lancs.; 44th Compy., Labour Corps.
Salonica, 1916-17, and part 1918. France, 1918. Doran Town, Brest village, Jackson's Ravine.
Special Constable, 1914-15.
Wounded once.

WATERS, Arthur Henry, Private.
Engineers' Department, Sandringham.
1 5th Norfolks.
Gallipoli. First Battle of Gaza; second Battle of Gaza. Palestine Campaign.
Stretcher-bearer.
Mentioned in Despatches.
Wounded once.

WATTS, Victor Albert, Corporal.
Under Gamekeeper, Congham, Sandringham.
Joined, 1st September, 1914.
Lance-Corporal, Corporal.
1 5th Norfolks; 54th Machine Gun Battalion.
Infantryman and Machine Gunner.
Gallipoli. Egypt. Palestine. Suvla Bay, Siffie Hill, Medjil Habb. Suez Canal. Three Gaza battles, Tree Hill, etc. Ramleh, Raselin, etc.
Wounded once.

WAY, George Robert, Private.
Gamekeeper, Sandringham.
Joined, 27th November, 1916.
Yorkshire Regiment.
Ypres and St. Quentin.
Wounded once.

WEATHERLY, John Edward, 2nd Lieutenant.
Lamplighter (Windsor Castle), Lord Steward's Department.
Joined, 25th November, 1915.
2nd Lieutenant, 25th June, 1918.
Army Service Corps.
Royal Welsh Fusiliers; Royal Berkshire Regiment.
Steinbeck, Langemark, Pilgrim Ridge, Armentières, advance during September, 1918.
Wounded, 21-22nd September, 1918.

WEBBER, Raymond Sudeley, Brevet Lieut.-Colonel.
Gentleman-at-Arms.
Brevet Lieut.-Colonel, 1917.
Royal Welsh Fusiliers, August, 1914; Irish Guards, September, 1914.
Commanding Dep't, Royal Welsh Fusiliers.
Irish Guards, First Battle of Ypres; Commanded Battalion for a short period; Commandant, School of Instruction, 2nd Army, and Southern Army, Home Defence, 1916-17; Command, Dep't, London Command, 1918.
Wounded once.

WELLS, Albert Richard, Private.
Woods, Sandringham.
Joined, 10th May, 1917.
Machine Gun Corps.
Wounded once. Gassed.

WILSON, Tom, Private.
Windsor Royal Gardens.
Joined, 28th July, 1917.
Manchester Regiment, 53rd, 51st, 1/6th, 3rd.
France.
Gassed.

WING, George Clifford, Sergeant.
Windsor Royal Gardens.
Joined, 20th September, 1915.
Sergeant.
Machine Gun Corps.
Somme, Ypres, Arras. Archangel.
Wounded twice.

(C) SERVED IN A THEATRE OF WAR OR AFLOAT

KERMAN, G. Charles, Private.
Gentleman of H.M. Chapel Royal (St. James), Lord Chamberlain's Department.
oined, 30th April, 1917.
Royal Army Ordnance Corps.
British Expeditionary Force, Mesopotamia.

NEW, Quentin G. K., Lieut.-Colonel, D.S.O., M.V.O.
Gentleman-at-Arms.
Acting Full Colonel while Commandant of Mudros.
3rd Batt., Royal Scots Fusiliers, Officer Commanding; 1st Batt., King's Own Scottish Borderers, Officer Commanding; 87th Brigade (commanded); 29th Brigade (commanded); 7th Corps, B.E.F. (Area Commandant), Labour Corps (Group Commander).
Special service, Gallipoli, 1915; Helles, July-August, 1915; Suvla operations, August-September, 1915; Commandant, Mudros, September, 1915-February, 1916; France, 1917; Area Commandant, 7th Corps, October, 1917-March, 1918; Cambrai operations, November-December, 1918; engagements with the 9th Division in retirement, 21st March to 1st April, 1918; in command of 9th Labour Corps Headquarters to date.

LEN, Ernest Edward, Private.
Appleton Farm, Sandringham.
Joined, 10th December, 1915.
Machine Gun Corps.
Macedonian Front and Russia; Black Rock engagement; Grand Corande engagement; Pippe Ridge engagement.

NNISON, Joseph, Corporal.
Mole Destroyer, Sandringham.
Joined, 7th December, 1915.
Lance-Corporal, Corporal.
Royal Fusiliers; Somerset Light Infantry; Wiltshires.
France—Arras, Telegraph Hill, Wancourt, Ypres, Glencorse Wood, Inverness Copse, Passchendaele, St. Quentin.

ASKER, Edward, D.M. 2, Private.
Engineers' Department, Sandringham.
Joined, 10th December, 1915.
5th Canadian Siege Battery, Ammunition Column; 56th Division Mechanical Workshops.
Battle of the Somme, 1916; at the taking of Vimy, 1917; Ypres, and the taking of Passchendaele, 1917; Battles of Cambrai, Valenciennes, Mons, 1918.

ASKER, William, Private.
Farm, Sandringham.
Joined, September, 1914.
Army Service Corps.

ATHOW, Thomas, Private.
Carpenter's Labourer, Sandringham.
Joined, 20th November, 1915.
2nd Norfolks.
Sharabar, Bagdad, Kirzil, Robat, Mazarna, Kifui

BAILEY, Arthur B., Private.
Royal Mews.
Joined, 3rd July, 1918.
13th London Regiment (Kensingtons).
France.

BAILEY, Frederick James, Major.
Clerk to Master of the Household, Lord Steward's Department.
Joined, 23rd December, 1915.
Major, 20th February, 1920.
Military Intelligence, Egypt; Personal Staff, G.O.C., Egypt; Labour Corps.
Egyptian Expeditionary Force, December, 1915, to July, 1916; British Expeditionary Force, August, 1917, to October, 1918.

BARNES, William, Lance-Corporal.
Gardener, Sandringham.
Joined, 3rd April, 1915.
Lance-Corporal.
92nd Field Ambulance, Royal Army Medical Corps.
Somme, 1916; Ancre, 1916; Savoy, 1917; Nieuport, 1917; Ypres, 1917; Ayette, 1918; Sequehart, 1918; Avesnes, 1918.

H

(C) SERVED IN A THEATRE OF WAR OR AFLOAT

BARTLETT, Clarence, Staff-Sergeant.
Engineers' Department, Sandringham.
Joined, 15th July, 1916.
Staff-Sergeant.
Royal Army Ordnance Corps and Royal Garrison Artillery.
Artificer in Royal Garrison Artillery at Lens, Arras, Monchy, Inchy, Bourlon Wood, Remicourt, Le Cateau, Cambrai, Valenciennes, Mons.

BATTERBEE, George, Sergeant.
Sandringham.
Joined, 4th August, 1914.
5th Norfolks.
Corporal, Sergeant.
Suvla Bay. Gaza. Palestine.

BATTERBEE, Harry, Private.
Garden Mill House, Sandringham.
Joined, 7th December, 1915.
36th Batt., Royal Fusiliers; Labour Corps; and 743rd Area Employment Compy.
France—Nieuport sector, Cambrai and Somme Fronts; trench digging, carrying ammunition, etc., in forward area.

BENSTEAD, William Henry, Driver.
Sandringham.
Joined, December, 1915.
12th Essex Regiment, transferred to M.G.C.
Vimy Ridge, Arras, Ypres, 1917. Embarked for Italy, 1917. Back to France, 1918.

BEST, Ernest Arthur, Gunner.
Windsor Royal Gardens.
Joined, 9th May, 1917.
Royal Garrison Artillery.
Ypres, Arras, Kemmel.

BEST, W., Driver.
Windsor Royal Gardens.
Joined 14th June, 1915.
Royal Field Artillery, 177th Brigade.
Somme, Ypres, Arras, Loos.

BIRD, Jack, Private.
Groom to Estate Agent, Sandringham.
Joined, 5th May, 1915.
Royal Army Veterinary Corps, France.
Rouen.

BLACKMAN, Charles, Private.
Porter, Lord Chamberlain's Department, Windsor Castle.
1st Bucks Battalion; 2/1st Bucks Battalion; 2/4th Oxon and Bucks.
Somme, Cambrai, Third Battle of Ypres, March Retreat St. Quentin Front, and the Advance.

BLAKE, Alexander, Private.
Garden Labourer, Balmoral.
Joined, 5th August, 1914.
2nd Scottish Horse; 13th Black Watch (R.H.).
Gallipoli, 1915; Egypt, 1915-16; Salonica, 1916-18; France, 1918-19. Le Catelet, Nurlu, Le Cateau, Monsau, Semousies, Villers Farm, Fontain.

BLAKE, William, Private.
Sandringham.
Joined, 5th August, 1914 (enlisted 1902, 3 years with the Colours, 9 in Reserve).
1st Batt., Norfolks.
Mons, Marne and Somme.

BOLD, C. W., Private.
Royal Mews.
Joined, 13th February, 1916.
3rd Hussars; 3rd County of London Yeomanry; Machine Gun Corps.
France—Battles of Cambrai and Douai.

BOSHER, Frederick, Private.
Kitchen Porter, Lord Steward's Department.
Joined, 12th February, 1917.
12th North Staffords.
Ypres, Somme, Armentières.

BOUGHEN, Leslie Vincent, 2nd Aircraftsman.
Sandringham.
Joined, 3rd June, 1918.
R.A.F.
2nd Aircraftsman, No. 1 Flight.
R.A.F. in France.

(C) SERVED IN A THEATRE OF WAR OR AFLOAT

BOWLBY, Sir Anthony, Major-General.
Surgeon-in-Ordinary, Lord Chamberlain's Department.
Full Colonel, 1914; Surgeon General, 1915; Major-General, 1918.
Army Medical Service.
Consulting Surgeon, British Expeditionary Force, September, 1914; attached G.H.Q. for Service at Front; Advising Consulting Surgeon, British Armies in France, attached G.H.Q.; present at First, Second and Third Battle of Ypres; Battle of Somme, 1916; Arras, 1917; German attack, March-April, 1918; British offensive, August-November, 1918.
K.C.M.G., K.C.V.O., C.B.

BOYLE, James, Private.
Gardens, Sandringham.
Joined, 3rd April, 1915.
92nd Field Ambulance, Royal Army Medical Corps.
Somme, Beaumont Hamel, 1916; Retirement, Arras - St. Quentin; Nieuport Coast Battle, Ypres, 1917; Arras flank; and continued fighting from Hangard to Avesnes, 1918.

BRIDGES, Ernest, Sergeant.
Woods, Sandringham.
Joined, 21st July, 1915.
Sergeant.
Norfolk Yeomanry and Machine Gun Corps.
On the Somme, Ypres, Lens, Cambrai, Arras.

BRIDGES, William Henry, Private.
Under Gamekeeper, Sandringham.
Joined, 5th July, 1915.
Royal Engineers.
Somme, Arras, Armentières, Ypres.

BRINTON, John Chaytor, Brevet Lieut.-Colonel.
Gentleman Usher, Lord Chamberlain's Department.
Brevet Lieut.-Colonel, 1st January, 1919.
2nd Life Guards, 5th October, 1914; Staff Cavalry Corps, June, 1915; Staff 8th Corps, March, 1916.
Flanders, October, 1914-15; First and Second Battle of Ypres; Battle of Lens (Loos, Hulluch), September, 1915; operations on the Somme, 1916.
Staff, G.H.Q. Forces of Great Britain from 4th September, 1916.
Mentioned in Despatches.

BROWN, F. G., Private.
Windsor Farms.
Joined, 15th February, 1917.
3rd Royal Berks; 1 4th Royal Berks.
France. Belgium. Italy. Ypres, Vimy Ridge, Asiago.

BRUCE, David, Private.
Stableman, Balmoral.
Joined, 18th March, 1916.
1 7th Gordon Highlanders; 11th Entrenching Battalion.
France, 1916; Somme, 1916; Ireland, 1917.

BUCHANAN, Andrew Sinclair, Captain.
Clerk, Lord Chamberlain's Office.
Captain, 1st June, 1916.
9th London Regiment (Q.V.R.); Labour Corps.
Commanded 806th Area Employment Compy., Labour Corps, Egyptian Expeditionary Force, 6th November, 1917, to 24th February, 1918.
Commanded No. 2 Group, Area Employment Companies, Labour Corps, Egyptian Expeditionary Force, 25th February, 1918, to 15th January, 1919.

BURN, Charles Rosdew, Colonel.
H.M.'s Royal Bodyguard. A.D.C. to His Majesty. Lord Chamberlain's Department.
General Staff Officer.
Carried Despatches from War Office and back.
To Commander-in-Chief in France; to Egypt; to Dardanelles (1915); to Italian Front; to Russian Front.

CAMBRIDGE, The Marquis of, Lieut.-Colonel.
Governor and Constable of Windsor Castle, Lord Chamberlain's Department.
1st Life Guards.
Later at General Headquarters
Served in Flanders, First Battle of Ypres, 1914; from the end of 1915 to April, 1916, appointed Military Secretary, G.H.Q., with rank of Brigadier-General; 1915, Assistant Military Secretary, War Office.
Order of Leopold, Grand Cross and Belgian Croix de Guerre, Commander Legion d'Honneur.

(C) SERVED IN A THEATRE OF WAR OR AFLOAT

CAMPBELL, Henry Hervey, Vice-Admiral.
Groom-in-Waiting, Lord Chamberlain's Department.
H.M.S. *Bacchante.*
Cruiser Force " C " in the North Sea; Heligoland Bight; employed by Admiralty in the Foreign Trade Department of the Foreign Office.
C.B., 1917.

CANNON, John Henry, Gunner.
Windsor Royal Gardens.
Joined, 22nd September, 1915.
Royal Horse Artillery.
Messines, Ypres, Newport.

CAPELL, Ernest Phillip, Private.
Royal Mews.
Joined, June, 1918.
Royal Army Service Corps.
France. Belgium.

CARTER, John Richard Charles, Lieutenant, Royal Naval Reserve.
Master of H.M. Yacht, " Britannia."
Joined, 14th July, 1916.
Hospital Yacht, " Sunbeam "; Armed Trawlers, " Touraco " and " Sea Monarch."
Master of H.M. Hospital Yacht, " Sunbeam," from May, 1915, to April, 1916, Dardanelles, Mediterranean and India. 14th July to November, 1916, on Patrol Work (Shetland Islands); November, 1916, to February, 1917, Minesweeping, etc., at Dover. February, 1917, to January, 1918, Minesweeping, escorting, or Patrolling at Portland. March, 1918, Engagement with Submarine.
Promoted to Lieutenant, Royal Naval Reserve.
D.S.C.

CHAPPLE, Sir John H. G., Paymaster, Rear-Admiral
Secretary of the Privy Purse.
H.M.S. *Agincourt*, Grand Fleet; H.M. Coast Guard, Londonderry; Admiralty.
North Sea.
Paymaster Director-General, Admiralty.
K.C.B.

CHEYNE, William Watson, Surgeon Rear-Admiral, R.N.
Hon. Surgeon-in-Ordinary to His Majesty, Lord Chamberlain's Department.
Joined, August, 1914.
Stationed at Chatham, visiting other places as required. Once sent to Malta (June, 1915) and to Dardanelles (October, 1915), on both occasions in Hospital Ship *Rewa.*
K.C.M.G., 1915.

CLARK, F., Trooper.
Windsor Royal Gardens.
Joined, 30th January, 1918.
2nd Life Guards; Machine Gun Guards.
Gommecourt, Albert Sequart, Belingluese, St. Quentin, Bray, Eppey.

CLAYSON, Alfred, 2nd Aircraftsman.
Carpenter, Sandringham.
Joined, 1st November, 1914.
1/5th Norfolks.
Royal Air Force.
Salonica Forces. Struma and Dorian Fronts.

CODLIN, Edgar, Private.
Gardens, Sandringham.
Joined, 13th December, 1917.
London Rifles.
France.

COLLIE, Wolseley, Private.
Garden Labourer, Balmoral.
Joined, August 5th, 1914.
2nd Scottish Horse; transferred to 13th Black Watch (R.H.), October, 1916.
Gallipoli, from August to December, 1915; Egypt, from December to October, 1916; Salonica, from October, 1916, to June, 1918; France, from June, 1918, to February 1919; Le Catelet Nurlu, Le Cateau, Villars Farms, Semousiers, Landrecies.

COLLISON, Preston, Gunner.
Sandringham.
Joined, July, 1916.
Royal Garrison Artillery.
3rd Battle of Ypres; the Battle of Cambrai.

(C) SERVED IN A THEATRE OF WAR OR AFLOAT

COMBER, Ernest, Rifleman.
Under Butler, Lord Steward's Department.
Joined, 1st September, 1914.
Sergeant.
1st Surrey Rifles.
Festubert, Givenchy, Loos, Somme.

COOK, George, Driver.
Windsor Royal Gardens.
Joined, 20th March, 1915.
R.F.A.
France.

COUTTS, Charles William, Trooper.
Roads Labourer, Balmoral.
Joined, 5th August, 1914.
1 2nd Batt., Scottish Horse, attached to 13th Black Watch about December, 1916.
Egypt. Salonika. France. General service.

CRITCHETT, George Montague, Captain.
Clerk, Lord Chamberlain's Office.
Captain, 1st June, 1916.
9th London Regiment (Q.V.R.); Machine Gun Corps; Chinese Labour Corps; Labour Corps.
Commanded 99th Compy. Chinese Labour Corps, Lines of Communication, France; Adjutant, Headquarters, 19th Labour Group, Lines of Communication, France, 20th July, 1917, to 7th July, 1918; War Office (A.G. 4 F), 7th October, 1918, to 1st January, 1919 (when demobilised).

CROSS, Herbert, Private.
Sandringham.
Joined, 11th November, 1915.
2nd Garrison, Northumberland Fusiliers.
Mesopotamia and India.

CROSS, Percy Donald, Rifleman.
Woods, Sandringham.
Joined, 24th May, 1917.
3rd Batt., Rifle Brigade.
Cambrai, Lens. British Advance, 1918.

CROWE, Francis Harold, Private.
Groom (Shires), Farm, Sandringham.
1 5th Norfolks.
Gallipoli Peninsula. Suez Canal. Egypt. Palestine. Gaza, 28th March, 1917, 19th April, 1917, 2nd November, 1917; final operations, 19th September, 1918.

CRUISE, Richard Robert, Captain, R.A.M.C. (T.).
Surgeon Oculist Extraordinary to H.M. The King, Lord Chamberlain's Department.
Joined, 8th August, 1914.
Royal Army Medical Corps.
France—Front line from Passchendaele to Peronne.
Opthalmic Specialist, 3rd London General Hospital, Wandsworth. Sole charge of upwards of 300 beds.
C.V.O.

DANIELS, Ernest James, Private.
Under Keeper, Sandringham.
1 5th Norfolks.
Gallipoli, 1915. Egypt, 1916.

DANIELS, George, Lance-Corporal.
Sandringham.
Joined, 4th August, 1914.
1st Garrison Batt., Essex Regiment.
Lance-Corporal.
Egypt. Palestine. Salonika. Sudan.

DANIELS, William Albert.
Sandringham.
Enlisted 1902. On Reserve at the time war broke out. Mobilised 4th August, 1914.
1st Norfolk Regiment.
Retreat of Mons. Loos. Somme. Ypres.

DAVIDSON, Leslie, Colonel.
Gentleman Usher, Lord Chamberlain's Department.
Served as Inspecting Officer for the Central Association of Volunteer Regiments in England, 1914.
In 1915 he went to France, and commanded successively Base Camps at Etaples and at Rouen, in his own rank of Colonel, Royal Artillery.
Died at Rouen, August, 1915.

(C) SERVED IN A THEATRE OF WAR OR AFLOAT

DAW, Frederick, Private.
Assistant Shepherd, Farm, Sandringham.
Joined, 12th July, 1916.
13th Queen's Royal West Surreys.
Somme; Belgian Front, Ypres; St. Quentin, Arras.

DAW, Robert John, Private.
Woods, Sandringham.
Joined, 13th June, 1916.
2nd Batt., Duke of Cornwall's Light Infantry.
Eastern Macedonia. Russia.
Transport Driver.

DAWS, Herbert, Private.
Wolferton Farm, Sandringham.
1 5th Norfolks.
On Transport, Eastern theatre.
Took part in Gaza battle, and Nablus.

DAWSON OF PENN, The Lord, Major-General.
Physician in Ordinary.
Joined, November, 1914.
Consulting Physician to the Army.
France.
Colonel, 1914, Major-General, 1917.
C.B., K.C.M.G.

DEAL, William George, Rifleman.
Assistant in Silver Pantry, Lord Steward's Department.
Joined, 7th September, 1914.
Sergeant.
6th London Rifles; transferred to Machine Gun Corps.
Festubert, Givenchy, Loos, Somme, Messines Ridge, Cambrai.

DEAN, James, Lance-Corporal.
Assistant Gardener, Balmoral.
Joined, 7th September, 1914.
Private to Lance-Corporal.
7th Gordon Highlanders.
France from 2nd May, 1915, to 24th March, 1916.
Rheumatic Fever, 1916.

DEAVES, George, Sergeant.
Thoroughbred Stallion Man, Stud, Sandringham.
Lance-Corporal, Lance-Sergeant, Full Sergeant.
1 5th Norfolks.
Gallipoli.

DICKINSON, Leslie John Bennach, Corporal.
Royal Mews.
Joined, 14th October, 1915.
Berks Yeomanry.
Corporal, Acting-Sergeant.
Egypt. Palestine. Gaza. Beersheba. W. Sheriah, Rafa, Remleh, Ludd, Jaffa. Arras, Douai, Ypres, Courtrai, Dickebosch, Menin, Passchendaele.

DOWNING, G., Private.
Royal Mews.
Joined, June, 1918.
Royal Army Service Corps (M.T.).
Mesopotamia. Persia.

DREW, Thomas, Private.
Labourer, Farm, Sandringham.
Joined, 25th May, 1915.
Royal Engineers.
France and Belgium—Somme, Arras, Hargicourt, Soissons, Ypres, Kemmel.

DUNCAN, William Francis, Private.
Farm Labourer, Abergeldie Mains.
Joined, 5th August, 1914.
1/7th Gordon Highlanders.
Neuve Chapelle, 1915; Loos, 1915.

DUNGER, Albert, Corporal.
Sandringham.
Joined, 1914.
1/5th Norfolk and 1st Essex Regiment.
Corporal.
Gallipoli, Egypt and France.
Prisoner of War.

DYE, John, Corporal.
Sandringham.
Joined, 18th January, 1915.
37th Reserve Park, R.A.S.C.; 800 Company.
Corporal.
Salonica (3 years). South Russia (7 months).

(C) SERVED IN A THEATRE OF WAR OR AFLOAT

EAST, Arthur Harding, Leading Mechanic.
King's Waterman, Lord Chamberlain's Department.
Joined, August, 1914.
From Air Mechanic, First Class, to Leading Mechanic.
Royal Naval Air Service.
Dunkirk, 1915. Dardanelles, 1915 to 1917. Salonika, 1917 to 1918.
Distinguished Service Medal.

EDMONSTONE, James, Corporal.
Upholsterer, Lord Chamberlain's Department.
Corporal.
5th Royal Scots; Royal Air Force.
France.

EDWARDS, James Hayward, Private.
Gamekeeper, Windsor. Deputy Rangers.
Joined, 8th December, 1915.
Royal Army Service Corps (M.T.).
Somme, Vimy Ridge, Ypres, Armentières, Cambrai.

ELMER, Arthur, Corporal.
Porter, Lord Chamberlain's Department.
Joined, 3rd September, 1914.
Sergeant, Bedfordshire Regiment, November, 1914. Corporal, Royal Army Service Corps, November, 1917.
Bedfordshire Regiment; Royal Army Service Corps.
Served with Bedfordshire Regiment on the Somme, 1916. Invalided, October, 1916, and transferred to Royal Army Service Corps. Remainder of service as Chief Clerk at Supply Depot, Felixstowe.

EMMERSON, Albert, Guardsman.
Gardener, Windsor Royal Gardens.
Joined, 15th November, 1915.
Irish Guards.
Ypres, 1917, Cambrai, Arras, Grand Offensive, 1918.

ERSKINE, Arthur Edward, Lieut.-Colonel.
Equerry.
Joined, June, 1919.
Royal Artillery.
Major, 1914. Brevet Lieut.-Colonel, 1918.
Ypres, Somme, Cambrai.
D.S.O. Mentioned four times in Despatches.

EVANS, Eric John Glynne, Lieutenant.
Private Secretary's Office.
Joined, January, 1916.
Devonshire Regiment.
Lieutenant.
Palestine.

FERGUSON, James Wilson, Private.
Under Gamekeeper, Balmoral.
Joined, 22nd February, 1915.
3rd Gordon Highlanders; 1st Gordon Highlanders; Royal Engineers.
Loos, 1915; Somme, 1916; Beaumont Hamel, 1916; Arras, 1917; Zonebecke, 1917.

FERGUSON, William, Private.
Woods Labourer, Balmoral.
Joined, 5th August, 1914.
Territorial Force. 1 7th Gordon Highlanders; 2 7th Gordon Highlanders; 4th Gordon Highlanders; Machine Gun Corps.
France.

FFOLKES, Francis Arthur, Lieut.-Colonel, S.C.F.
Chaplain-in-Ordinary to H.M. The King, Lord Chamberlain's Department.
S.F., E.M.B., C.F., E.M.B., S.E.B. (amalgamated).
S.C.F., 74th Division (Dismounted Yeomanry).
S.C.F., Kantara and Canal Zone, E.E.F.
Gallipoli, Suez, Jordan, Balah, Sollum, Palestine (from before the Second Battle of Gaza to taking of Jerusalem).
Lieut.-Colonel—*i.e.*, Second Class, S.C.F.
Mentioned in Despatches.

FORSYTH, H. C., Divl. Sergt.-Major.
Piper to the King.
Joined, 5th February, 1915.
14th Argyll and Sutherland Highlanders.
Served in France as Divisional Sergeant-Major to the 40th Divisional Infantry Base Depot, 6th June, 1916, to 1st December, 1917; Regimental Sergeant-Major (Training Centre), No. 11 Convalescent Depot, Buchy, France, December, 1917, to January, 1919; Divisional Sergeant-Major.

FRANKS, George, Private.
Royal Mews.
Joined, March, 1915.
Royal East Kent Mounted Rifles.
Western Front.

FREEMAN, George William.
Windsor Royal Gardens.
Joined, 22nd February, 1915.
3rd Royal Berks; Royal Warwicks; Hampshire Regiment.
France. Egypt.

FRYATT, Charles John, Driver.
Assistant Keeper, Sandringham.
Joined, 5th July, 1915.
Royal Engineers.
Vimy Ridge, Cambrai. Defence work.

GAME, T., Corporal.
Royal Mews.
Joined, 24th April, 1915.
1st City of London Yeomanry, and 103rd Batt. Machine Gun Corps.
Corporal.
Egypt, Salonika, Palestine, France, Gaza, Beersheba, Jerusalem.

GARLICK, George, Private.
Windsor Royal Gardens.
Berks Regiment.
Salonika, 1916-19.

GARNER, Harold, Private.
Gardens, Sandringham.
Joined, 4th August, 1914, to 18th August, 1914; 18th November, 1914, to 15th October, 1917.
Sergeant.
1 5th Norfolks; 5th Duke of Wellington's.
France—Somme, 8th August and 16th December, 1916.

GASCOIGNE, Ernest Frederick Orby, C.M.G., D.S.O., Brigadier-General.
Gentleman-at-Arms, Royal Bodyguard, Lord Chamberlain's Department.
Brevet Lieut.-Colonel, 1st January, 1916; Temp. Brigadier-General, February, 1918; Hon. Brigadier-General, February, 1918.
Served on Staff.
Dardanelles Campaign, March, 1915, to December, 1915. D.A.Q.M.G., then A.Q.M.G., G.H.Q., Mediterranean Expeditionary Force.
Egypt, January, 1916, to December, 1916, Egyptian Expeditionary Force.
Palestine, December, 1916, to January, 1918.
D.A.Q.M.G. (Brigadier-General), Eastern Force.
Then Assistant to D.A.M.G. (Brigadier-General), G.H.Q., Egyptian Expeditionary Force.
Aldershot, 4th August, 1914, to March, 1915.
C.M.G. Order of St. Anne, 2nd Class.

GAULD, Peter George, Private.
Gardener, Balmoral.
Joined, 15th January, 1916.
Gordon Highlanders; Queen's Own Oxford Hussars.
Somme, 1916; Beaumont Hamel, 1916; Offensive, 1917; Offensive, 1918.

GENT, W., Private.
Farm Labourer, Sandringham.
Joined, 4th April, 1916.
34th Royal Fusiliers, France; 102nd Labour Compy., France; 778th Area Employment Compy., France; 992nd Area Employment Compy., France; 726th Labour Compy., France.

(C) SERVED IN A THEATRE OF WAR OR AFLOAT

GIBBS, Arthur.
Waterman to His Majesty, Lord Chamberlain's Department.
Joined, 6th December, 1916.
Corporal.
Inland Water Transport, Royal Engineers.
France.

GLEICHEN, Lord Edward, Major-General, K.C.V.O., C.B., C.M.G., D.S.O.
Equerry.
Commanded 15th Infantry Brigade; Commanded 37th Infantry Division.
Major-General.
Ministry of Information.
Actions at Mons Retreat, Le Cateau, Marne, First Battle of the Aisne, La Bassée, First Battle of Ypres, First Battle of Somme.

GODEFROI, Jocelyn, Lieutenant.
Clerk, Lord Chamberlain's Office.
Joined, 11th March, 1916.
Lieutenant, 8th February, 1917.
2nd Batt., Artists' Rifles (O.T.C.); Royal Army Ordnance Corps.
Commissioned in Royal Army Ordnance Corps, 8th November, 1916, and posted to Stirling.
With Royal Army Ordnance Corps in France, March to December, 1918.

GODFREY, William, Lance-Corporal.
Horseman, Farm, Sandringham.
Joined, 15th May, 1915.
Lance-Corporal.
Royal Engineers.
Somme, Arras, Hargicourt, Somme, Armentières, Soissons, Kemmel, Ypres, St. Quentin.
Meritorious Service Medal.

GODFREY-FAUSSETT, Sir Bryan Godfrey, Captain, R.N. (retired).
Equerry.
H.M. Armed Yacht *Thistle*.
Patrol work.
East Coast of Scotland.

GOODING, Henry, Squadron-Quartermaster-Sergeant.
Yeoman of the Guard.
Joined, 10th March, 1915.
To Regimental-Sergeant-Major.
Remount Department.
Four years in France.

GOODMAN, Herbert, Pioneer.
Sandringham.
Joined, March 2nd, 1917.
King Royal Rifles and C.P.S., Royal Engineers.
France; Germany.

GRANARD, The Earl of, Lieut.-Colonel.
Master of the Horse.
Reserve of Officers, Scots Guards; 5th Batt., The Royal Irish Regiment, and Military Secretary to Commander-in-Chief, British Salonika Force.
Landing at Suvla, August, 1915, and subsequent operations; Salonika, 1915; Serbia, to July, 1917.
Officer of the Legion of Honour; Commander of the White Eagle of Serbia (with swords; Commander of the Order of the Redeemer of Greece.
Mentioned in Despatches four times.

GRANT, Arthur Rowland Harry, The Rev.
Domestic Chaplain to The King, Lord Chamberlain's Department.
Joined, 10th January, 1916, and 9th July, 1918.
12th General Hospital, Rouen; 2nd Queen's and 1st S. Staffs.; 6th Cavalry Brigade Headquarters.
Battle of Somme, July, 1916; Battle of Amiens, August, 1918; Battle of Le Cateau, September, 1918.

GREEN, Henry.
Windsor Royal Gardens.
Joined, November, 1916.
Royal Berks.
France.

GREEN, James Edward, Private.
Team-man, Farm, Sandringham.
Joined, 25th March, 1916.
34th Batt., Royal Fusiliers; Labour Corps.
France and Belgium.

(C) SERVED IN A THEATRE OF WAR OR AFLOAT

GRIMES, James, Lance-Corporal.
Sandringham.
Joined, October, 1916.
2nd Norfolk Regiment.
Mesopotamia. N.W. Frontier of India.

GRIMES, John, Private.
Stud, Sandringham.
Joined, 30th March, 1916.
6th Bedfords; Herts.
Somme, Bouy-Couy, Courdry, Arras, Ashley-le-Grange, Gousencourt. Belgium. Albert.

GUNN, John.
Yeoman of the Guard.
Joined, January, 1915.
Chinese Labour Corps.
Served in France in command of Chinese Labour Corps.
D.C.M.
Captain.

GUNNING, G. J., Gunner.
Royal Mews.
Joined, 5th August, 1914.
Royal Field Artillery (Territorials).
Served in France.
Died, November, 1918.

HARRIS, Percy, Private.
Royal Mews.
Joined, 10th February, 1916.
Army Veterinary Corps; 16th West Riding Labour Corps.
Arras, Vimy.

HARROD, Ernest Lewis, Corporal.
Horseman, Sandringham.
Joined, 26th February, 1917.
Corporal.
Royal Horse Artillery.
Served with Royal Horse Artillery, 20th Brigade Headquarters; Egyptian Expeditionary Force, Egypt.

HARROD, William, Corporal.
Gardener, Park House, Sandringham.
Joined, 16th October, 1916.
Corporal.
2 6th Norfolks.
France. Served with the 180th P.O.W. Compy. Escort.

HAYWOOD, Clifford, Sergeant
Royal Mews.
Joined, 28th August, 1914.
Royal Engineers, Motor Cyclist Section.
France.

HEALEY, Albert Edward, Sapper.
King's Waterman, Lord Chamberlain's Department.
Joined, 3rd March, 1917.
Sapper to Barge Captain, March, 1919.
Royal Engineers, Inland Water Transport.
Transportation of Ammunition on French and Belgian Canals.

HESTER, George.
Windsor Royal Gardens.
Joined, August, 1914.
Royal Berks.
France and Belgium.

HIGGINS, George, Rifleman.
Porter, Lord Chamberlain's Department, Windsor Castle.
Joined, 31st August, 1914.
King's Royal Rifles
France, July, 1915. Loos, Ypres, and various parts of the line.
Taken Prisoner, Ypres, 19th February, 1916.

HILL, Ernest George, Sergeant-Major.
Royal Mews.
Joined, 21st September, 1914.
Royal Horse and Field Artillery.
Corporal, Sergeant, Quarter-Master-Sergeant, Sergeant-Major.
Loos, Somme, Arras, Ypres, Cambrai, Arras Nearch, Soissons, Hulloch, Tournai.
M.M. and Bar.

(C) SERVED IN A THEATRE OF WAR OR AFLOAT

HOUCHEN, Charles, Private.
Gardens, Sandringham.
Joined, 30th July, 1915.
Royal Horse Artillery.
Mesopotamia.

HOULDEN, John William Freeman, Private.
Royal Mews.
Joined, 6th October, 1914.
23rd Royal Fusiliers; transferred to Royal Army Service Corps.
Cambrai, Festubert, Givenchy, Lonsez, Vimy.

HOWELL, William, Private.
Sandringham.
Joined, 16th February, 1917.
London Regiment.
Egypt.

HUDSON, Ernest Louis, Private.
Carpenter's Yard, Sandringham.
1 5th Norfolks.
Dardanelles, Suvla Bay Landing, 1915. Palestine, Gaza.
Wounded once.
Died at Felixstowe, 1918, from Influenza, through health being lowered through Service conditions.

HUGHES, William Alfred, Gunner.
Windsor Farms.
Joined, 5th February, 1917.
Royal Field Artillery and Royal Garrison Artillery.
Ypres, Cambrai, 1918.

HUMPHREY, Charles, Private.
Sandringham.
Joined, 9th September, 1914.
1 5th Norfolks.
Gallipoli.

HUNLOKE, Philip, Major.
Groom-in-Waiting, Lord Chamberlain's Department.
Joined, 1st October, 1914.
Staff. G.S.O. 3.
King's Messenger, 1st October, 1914, to 20th November, 1915. Staff, G.S.O. 3, 1st Army, 20th November, 1915, to September, 1917.
A.D.C., G.O.C., 1st Army, September, 1917, to June, 1918.
Mentioned in Despatches. Chevalier Legion d'Honneur. Order of St. Stanislaus, 2nd Class.

INCHBOLD, Percy, Private.
Porter, Lord Chamberlain's Department, Windsor Castle.
Joined, 9th November, 1915.
Royal Berks Regiment; East Kent Regiment.
France and Egypt. Somme, Vimy Ridge. Beersheba.

JACOBS, Arthur Henry, Driver.
Royal Mews.
Joined, 18th April, 1915.
Royal Field Artillery.
Somme. Western Front.

JONES, John, Farrier-Quarter-Master-Sergeant.
Royal Mews.
Joined, 14th April, 1915.
Royal Horse Artillery.
Gallipoli. Beaumont Hamel, Somme, Arras, Monchy, Steinbeck.
Mentioned in Despatches.

JONES, John Edward, Private.
Royal Mews.
Joined, 5th March, 1917.
Devonshire Regiment.
France.

KEEN, George, Driver, Lance-Corporal.
Windsor Farms.
Joined, 1st September, 1914.
Royal Engineers.
Lance-Corporal.
Albert, Arras, Loos, Quarries, Hohenzollern, Ovillers, Somme, Cambrai, Nurlu, Epehy.

KNIBBS, Arthur, Gunner.
Windsor Royal Gardens.
Joined, 26th January, 1915.
Royal Field Artillery.
Mesopotamia. India.

KYTE, Henry Frederick, Private.
Royal Mews.
Joined, 20th November, 1916.
Royal Flying Corps; Royal Army Veterinary Corps
France.

(C) SERVED IN A THEATRE OF WAR OR AFLOAT

LAIRD, William, Private.
Joiner, Balmoral.
Joined, 10th September, 1914.
7th and 6th Gordon Highlanders.
Festubert, 1915; Arras, 1917; Ypres, 1917; Bapaume, 1918; La Bassée, 1918; Marne, 1918; Scarpe, 1918.

LAMBERT, Albert William, Private.
Royal Mews.
Joined, 15th June, 1915.
Royal Army Service Corps; 1/8th Hants.
Egypt. Palestine.

LAMBTON, Sir William, Major-General.
Groom-in-Waiting, Lord Chamberlain's Department.
Brigadier-General, 1914; Major-General, 1915.
Staff Army.
August, 1914, to September, 1917. Mons, Marne, 1914; Ypres, 1914-15; Somme, 1916; Arras, 1917.
Military Secretary to C.M.C., August, 1914, to September, 1915.
Commanded 4th Division, September, 1914, to September, 1917.
C.V.O., 1914; C.B., 1915; K.C.B., 1918.

LASCELLES, George Reginald, Lieut.-Colonel.
Yeoman of the Guard.
Joined, 28th November, 1914.
Lieut.-Colonel.
Royal Fusiliers.
Commanded 16th Batt., Royal Fusiliers.
Area Commandant Behen and Cavillon (Somme), B.E.F., France.

LAWLEY, The Hon. Ursula Mary, Serving Sister, Order of St. John of Jerusalem.
Maid of Honour to Her Majesty the Queen.
November, 1914, Hôpital Dumaresq for French Soldiers; February, 1915, Border Hospital, Dunkerque; May, 1915, No. 14 General Military Hospital, Wimereux.
R.R.C. Mentioned in Despatches.

LAWS, Herbert, Private.
Gardens, Sandringham.
Joined, 3rd April, 1915.
Royal Army Medical Corps; 2nd East Lancs. Field Ambulance; 3rd Middlesex Regiment; 97th Sanitary Section.
Gallipoli. Egypt. Salonika—Struma, Dovean.

LINES, James William, Private.
Labourer, Carpenters' Department, Sandringham.
13th Labour Batt.; Queen's Royal West Surreys; 93rd Labour Batt.; 833rd Area Employment Compy.
Labour Overseas only.

LINES, Walter Leonard, Sergeant.
Sandringham.
Joined, May, 1915.
6th Batt., Royal Fusiliers; 2nd Batt., Essex Regiment.
Sergeant, 1917.
Mesopotamia. India.

LUCAS, Hugh Noakes, Private.
Royal Mews.
Joined, 1st October, 1914.
Motor Transport, Royal Army Service Corps, 8th Division Supply Column, 74th Company.
November, 1914, Second Battle of Ypres; Somme, 1915 and 1918.

MACRAE, Colin William, Major.
Yeoman of the Guard.
Joined, 30th November, 1914.
Major, 29th January, 1917.
Recruiting Officer, Scottish Command.
France. A.D.C. to Major-General Feltham, C.B., C.M.G., Commanding 39th Division. Served with the Division in the line held by the 5th Army till the Army was driven back in the great German attack on 21st March, 1918.

(C) SERVED IN A THEATRE OF WAR OR AFLOAT

MACRAE-GILSTRAP, John, Lieut.-Colonel.

Corps of Gentlemen-at-Arms, Lord Chamberlain's Department

Joined, 20th August, 1914. Appointed Recruiting Officer for Counties of Argyll and Bute.

Lieut.-Colonel, 2nd December, 1914.

11th (Service) Batt., Royal Highlanders (Black Watch); 38th Training Reserve Battalion; 202nd Infantry Battalion; 51st (Graduated) Batt., Gordon Highlanders.

France, 5th-22nd February, 1917. Attached to 1st Batt., Duke of Cornwall's Light Infantry, in the line at the village of Quinchy, on the La Bassée Canal.

Recruiting Officer for Counties of Argyll and Bute, 20th August to 1st December, 1914.

Appointed to Command the 11th (Service) Batt., Royal Highlanders (Black Watch).

Mentioned in *London Gazette*, 24th February, 1917, for "valuable services."

MARTEN, Alfred Vigor, Writer, R.N.

Privy Purse Office.

Joined, January, 1917.

H.M.S. *King George V.*

Grand Fleet.

MARTIN, James Evan Baillie, Major.

Sergeant-at-Arms.

Re-appointed from retired pay, 16th September, 1914.

A.P.M. from D.A.P.M.

10th Batt., King's Royal Rifle Corps; General Staff Officer for Musketry, 20th Division; D.A.P.M., 20th Division; A.P.M., 13th Corps.

All operations of 20th Division during War. Battle of Loos, September, 1915; Battle of the Somme, July to November, 1916; German Retreat to the Hindenburg Line, March, 1917; Battle of Passchendaele Ridge, July and August, 1917; Battle of Cambrai, November, 1917; Retreat on the Somme, March, 1918. With 13th Corps, Battle of the Selle, October, 1918; Battle of Maubeuge, November, 1918.

General Staff Officer for Musketry, 20th Division, 18th September, 1914, to 15th July, 1915.

D.A.P.M., 20th Division, 15th July, 1915, to 15th October, 1918.

A.P.M. 13th Corps, 15th October, 1918.

Twice mentioned in Despatches. Belgian Croix de Guerre. Chevalier de l'Ordre de Leopold.

MARTYN, Henry Linnington, M.B., B.S., London, F.R.C.S. Eng.

Surgeon Apothecary H.M. Household, Windsor, Lord Chamberlain's Department.

Joined, 16th August, 1914, to 4th August, 1915. 24th May, 1917, to 6th January, 1919.

Lieutenant to Captain, 24th November, 1917.

Royal Army Medical Corps.

In France with No. 12 General Hospital as Registrar and second Surgeon, August 22nd, 1914, to 4th August, 1915. Resigned commission to permit of partner serving.

Re-commissioned, 24th May, 1917, and served in France with No. 10 General Hospital from that date as Registrar and Surgical Specialist, to 6th September, 1918.

Recruiting Medical Officer, Windsor, September, 1915, to May, 1917.

Surgeon, Princess Christian Military Hospital, Englefield Green.

Assistant Surgeon, King Edward VII Hospital, Windsor, with military beds.

For three months Civil Surgeon in charge Coldstream Guards, Victoria Barracks, Windsor.

Wounded. Invalided home September, 1916, as result of sickness contracted on active service.

McGREGOR, Joseph, Private.

Garden Labourer, Balmoral.

Joined, 24th October, 1917.

Gordon Highlanders.

La Bassée Canal.

Prisoner of War.

McNAUGHTON, Wilfred, Corporal.

Kitchen Porter, Lord Steward's Department.

Joined, 5th August, 1914.

Private to Corporal.

Middlesex Regiment.

First Battle of Ypres; Loos, La Bassée, Armentières.

McONIE, Peter, Sergeant.

Gardens, Sandringham.

Joined, 4th August, 1914.

Sergeant, Acting-Sergeant-Major.

1 5th Norfolks; Machine Gun Corps.

Gallipoli—Kavak Tepe. France—Somme, Arras, Ypres, Cambrai.

(C) SERVED IN A THEATRE OF WAR OR AFLOAT

MELTON, Fredk. W. H., Private.
Sandringham.
Joined, 4th August, 1914.
1/5th Norfolk Regiment.
Gallipoli. Egypt.

MELTON, George, Sergeant.
Gardens, Sandringham.
Joined, 4th August, 1914.
Lance-Corporal, Corporal, Sergeant.
1 5th Norfolks.
Suvla Bay, 1915; Gaza, March, 1917; Gaza, April, 1917; Gaza, November, 1917.

MERRELL, David, Driver.
Royal Mews.
Joined, 1st October, 1914.
2 1st Berks; Royal Horse Artillery.
Plugstreet, Neuport, Ypres, Arras, Bouverie, Burnt Mill, Tantchines.

MERRIKIN, Herbert E., Private.
Sandringham.
Joined, 4th August, 1914.
1 5th Norfolks, 1 4th Devons.
Gallipoli. India.

MILNE, Sir Archibald Berkeley, Bt., Admiral.
Extra Equerry.
H.M.S. *Inflexible.*
Mediterranean.

MILNER, Edward, Major.
Gentleman-at-Arms.
10th Batt., King's Royal Rifle Corps; 16th Queen's Regiment (Royal West Surreys).
France, 1915. Trenches in front of Laventie. France, 1917. Area Stores Officer at Busseboom and Westoutre, Belgium. December, 1915, Commandant 4th Brigade, Young Officers' Compy., Moore Park, Kilworth, Co. Cork. Supt. Officer to a "Command Compy.," disbanded August, 1916. Served under A.P.M., Kingstown, Co. Dublin, 10 days during rebellion. Appointed 15th Training Batt., Seaford and Luton. Senior Major, 16th Queen's Regiment (Royal West Surreys), Farnham and Colchester; then to France, 16th May, 1917.

MINTER, Arthur, Sergeant.
Royal Mews.
Joined, 4th January, 1915.
Royal Field Artillery.
Sergeant.
Western Front. Balkans.

MITFORD, Bertram Reveley, C.B., C.M.G., D.S.O., Hon. Major-General.
Gentlemen-at-Arms.
Temp. Major-General; Hon. Major-General.
72nd Infantry Brigade; 42nd Division.
Commanded 72nd Infantry Brigade from September, 1914, to August, 1915, at home, and from August, 1915, to March, 1917, on Western Front.
Commanded 42nd Division from March, 1917, to October, 1917, on Western Front.
Battle of Loos, September, 1915. Gas attacks on Messines Ridge, 30th April and 17th June, 1916. The Somme, August and September, 1916. Passchendaele, August and September, 1917.
C.M.G.

MITFORD, William Kenyon, Colonel.
Gentleman-at-Arms.
Commandant, Petworth Remount Depôt, 4th August, 1914, till July, 1915; Draft-Conducting Officer from July, 1915, till July, 1917; Commandant at Zenephen, with B.E.F., 25th July, 1917, till 14th May, 1918.

MOLYNEUX, Frank, Private.
Gardens, Sandringham.
Joined, 3rd April, 1915.
Royal Army Medical Corps, Field Ambulance.
Gallipoli, September, 1915, to 29th December, 1915; Suez Canal, January, 1916, to May, 1916; Salonica, May, 1916, on Struma Front, to December, 1918.

MONTGOMERY, Herbert Francis, Lieutenant.
Private Secretary's Office.
Joined, February, 1916.
Black Watch; Argyll and Sutherland Highlanders.
Private to Lieutenant.
Salonika.

(C) SERVED IN A THEATRE OF WAR OR AFLOAT

MORLAND, J., Private.
Windsor Royal Gardens.
Joined, 4th December, 1914.
Oxford and Bucks Light Infantry.
Festubert, Vimy Ridge, Somme.

NEWTON, John William Marsdin, Brigadier-General.
Gentleman-at-Arms.
Brigadier-General (Hon.).
Volunteer Training Corps; Royal Artillery; Staff.
France, 1916-17, conducting drafts for various regiments; Belgium, 1917-18, as Area Commandant, at Ouderdom, near Ypres; in command Volunteer Training Corps, 1914; C.R.A. of 67th (Home Counties) Division, January, 1915, to January, 1916.

NURSE, Albert William.
Sandringham.
Joined, 4th August, 1914.
1 5th Norfolks.
Gallipoli. Suvla Bay.

PACE, Albert Edward, Gunner.
Royal Mews.
Joined, 7th September, 1914.
Royal Horse Artillery.
France.

PAINTER, Albert Henry, Rifleman.
Labourer, Sandringham.
Joined, 28th March, 1916.
2 6th Royal Sussex.
India.

PAINTER, William, Private.
Cowman, Sandringham Farm.
Joined, 29th March, 1916.
9th Queen's Royal West Surreys, and Labour Corps.
France.

PANTER, Albert E., Trumpeter.
Royal Mews.
Joined, August, 1914.
4th (Q.O.) Hussars.
France, 1915-1918.

PANTER, Joseph, Private,
Royal Mews.
Joined, 1914.
4th (Q.O.) Hussars.
Marne, Ypres 1914 and 1915, Hooge, Loos, Somme, Arras, Cambrai, Bourlon Wood, Amiens, Villers Bretonneaux.

PARNELL, Horace, Sergeant.
Royal Mews.
Joined, 19th March, 1915.
Royal Army Service Corps.
Lance-Corporal, Corporal, Sergeant.
Russia.

PARR, Robert, Sergeant.
Royal Mews.
Joined, 7th September, 1914.
Royal Field Artillery.
Sergeant.
Western Front. Balkans.

PATEMAN, James, Squadron-Sergeant-Major.
Yeoman of the Guard.
Joined, 10th February, 1915.
24th Squadron, Royal Army Service Corps.
No. 1 Base, Remount Depot, France.
Died in France.

PATIENCE, W., Driver.
Royal Mews.
Joined, 7th September, 1914
Royal Field Artillery.
France.

PATTINGALE, Albert Victor Emmerson, Private.
Carpenters' Yard, Sandringham.
Joined, 20th November, 1915.
Bedford Regiment; Duke of Cornwall's Own; Middlesex Regiment.
British Expeditionary Force, France.
Battle of Ypres, 31st July, 1917, to 24th October, 1917.

PEARCE, Edward James, Sergeant-Major.
Messenger, Lord Chamberlain's Office.
Joined, 15th October, 1915.
Corporal, 17th January, 1916; Sergeant, 14th July, 1916; Flight-Sergeant, 1st March, 1918; Sergeant-Major, 14th July, 1919.
Royal Flying Corps; Royal Air Force.
France, June, 1917, to January, 1919. Cambrai, November, 1918; Day Bombing of troops, aerodromes, etc.
School of Instruction at Reading, February, 1916, to May, 1917, in charge of billeting, etc., of 400 odd officers.
Disciplinary Sergeant to No. 3 Squadron, R.F.C.; Flight-Sergeant, No. 3 Squadron, R.F.C.; Sergeant-Major, No. 103 Squadron, R.A.F.

(C) SERVED IN A THEATRE OF WAR OR AFLOAT

PLAISTOWE, Thomas, Staff-Sergeant-Major.
Royal Mews.
Joined, 8th October, 1914.
Royal Army Service Corps (Horse Transport), attached 2 2nd South Midland Field Ambulance.
Staff-Sergeant-Major.
Somme, Beaumont, Arras, Ypres, Passchendaele, Fins, Cambrai, St. Quentin, Secmeries.

PONSONBY, The Rt. Hon. Sir Frederick, Lieut.-Colonel.
Keeper of Privy Purse.
Joined, August, 1914.
Grenadier Guards.
First Battle of Ypres. Liaison Officer, 7th Division
Mentioned in Despatches.

POUPART, Paul Henri, Private.
Cook, Lord Steward's Department.
Joined, 2nd August, 1914. French Army.
24me Section des Commis, ouvriers d'administration Français à Versailles, Seine et Oise.

PRENTICE, William, Sergeant.
Gardens, Sandringham.
Lance-Corporal, Corporal, Sergeant, Acting-Company-Sergeant-Major.
1 5th Norfolks.
Gallipoli, Suvla Bay. Egyptian and Palestine campaigns. Anafarta, 12th August, 1915; Gaza, March, 1917; Gaza, April, 1917; Gaza, November, 1917; Judean Hills, 1918.

RAINBOW, Ephraim James, Corporal.
Cabinet Maker, Lord Chamberlain's Department.
Joined, 27th December, 1914.
Corporal.
84th Field Compy. R.E. (20th Division); also 20th Division Band.
Battle of Loos. Stretcher-bearing at Battle of Gillemont, Les Bœufs, Langemarck, Eagle Trench objective, first Cambrai advance and retirement, St. Quentin retirement.

RAYMENT, Harry, Sergeant.
Porter, Lord Chamberlain's Department, Windsor Castle.
Joined, 15th September, 1914.
Lance-Corporal, December, 1915; Full Corporal, May, 1916; Sergeant, May, 1917.
Royal Army Medical Corps.
France. Base Hospital; Field Ambulance; Dressing Station at Epres, Meteran, Kemmel Hill, Brandhoek, Le Cateau, Caudry.
N.C.O. in charge of Officers' Division at No. 14 Stationary Hospital, France; also on No. 19 Field Ambulance.

RICHARDS, Martin J., 2nd Lieutenant.
H.M. The Queen's Household.
Joined, December, 1916.
Inns of Court Officers' Training Corps.
Royal Army Service Corps.
Palestine, 1918.

RIGBY, Hugh Mallinson, Colonel (Temp.), A.M.S.
Hon. Surgeon to the Household, Lord Chamberlain's Department.
Brevet Major, 1917; Brevet Lieut.-Colonel, 1918.
Royal Army Medical Corps and Army Medical Service.
Consultant to 2nd Army in France, April to November, 1916; Consulting Surgeon to the London District since January, 1917.

RIGBY, James, Regimental-Quartermaster-Sergeant.
Marshalman, Lord Steward's Department.
Joined, 15th September, 1914.
Promoted 2nd Class Warrant Officer, 29th January, 1915.
11th and 3rd Batts., Essex Regiment.
France, 28th August, 1915, to 15th October, 1916. 11th Batt., Essex Regiment. Loos, Ypres area; Somme, 1916.

ROBERTSON, William, Private.
Stoker, Balmoral.
Joined, 10th September, 1914.
1 7th Gordon Highlanders; 6 7th Gordon Highlanders.
Festubert, 1915; Somme, 1916; Beaumont Hamel, 1916; Vimy Ridge, 1917; Chemical Works, 1917; Ypres, 1917; Cambrai, 1917; Somme, 1918; La Bassée, 1918; Marne, 1918; Arras, 1918; Cambrai, 1918.

(C) SERVED IN A THEATRE OF WAR OR AFLOAT

RONDEST, Georges Maurice, Sergeant Chef de Section.
Pastry Cook, Lord Steward's Department.
224th Infanterie; 17th Infanterie (Territoriale); 24th Section, C.O.A.
France, 1914 to 1919.

ROSIER, Thomas, J., Gunner.
Windsor Royal Gardens.
Joined, 27th January, 1916.
Royal Garrison Artillery.
Passchendaele Ridge.

ROWLEY, The Hon. William Chambré, Lieut.-Colonel.
Royal Body Guard.
Hon. Lieut.-Colonel.
Royal Artillery.
France from 10th July, 1915, to December, 1916. Loos, September, 1915.
Croix de Guerre.

RYE, James Albert, Sergeant.
Messenger and Post Boy, Lord Steward's Department.
Joined, 1st September, 1914.
Lance-Corporal, Corporal, Sergeant.
1/5th Batt., Norfolk Regiment.
Gallipoli, 1915; Suvla Bay. Egypt, 1916. Palestine, 1917-18.

SANDERS, F., Driver.
Royal Mews.
Joined, 7th September, 1914.
Royal Field Artillery.
Second and third Battle of Ypres, Somme, Arras, Peronne, Passchendaele, Hooge, Lens.

SANDLE, John George, Private.
Engineers' Department, Sandringham.
Joined, 7th August, 1916.
Queen's Royal West Surrey Regiment; Royal Army Ordnance Corps.
Salonica—eight months.

SCHOFIELD, Harry Norton, Lieut.-Colonel, V.C
Gentleman-at-Arms.
To Lieut.-Colonel on being placed on retired list.
Remount Department.
Royal Artillery.
British Remount Commission in Canada and America, August, 1914, to March, 1915; D.A.D.R., Scottish Command, May, 1915, to August, 1915; Commandant on Line of Communication, France, 18th August, 1915, to 23rd April, 1917 (Temp. Lieut.-Colonel); in command of 73rd D.A.C., R.F.A., Home Forces, 23rd April, 1917, to 27th March, 1918.

SEABRIGHT, Thomas Andrew, Trooper.
Royal Mews.
Joined, 3rd September, 1914.
Royal Horse Guards.
Ypres, Loos, Hulloch, Somme.

SENTER, John William, Private.
Work in Pheasantries, Sandringham.
Joined, 14th October, 1916.
Labour Corps; Middlesex Regiment; Royal Fusiliers.
Two years in France and Belgium, mostly Somme area.

SMITH, Frederick, Private.
Gardens, Sandringham.
Joined, 10th June, 1916.
2nd Batt., Essex Regiment.
Somme, Arras and Ypres, 1917; Arras and Cambrai, 1918.

SMITH, Guy Vernon.
Priest-in-Ordinary to the King, Lord Chamberlain's Department.
Joined, October, 1914.
London Rifle Brigade.
Army Chaplain's Department.
France—with Bishop of London, April, 1915; Chaplain in the Line in France, January to end of July, 1917.
Macedonia—with Bishop of London, October, 1918.
Army Chaplain in England with London Rifle Brigade during 1914-15, and part of 1916, and part of 1918.
M.C., 1917; Greek Order of the Redeemer, 1918.

(C) SERVED IN A THEATRE OF WAR OR AFLOAT

SMITH, William, Private.
Engineers' Department, Sandringham.
Joined, 5th August, 1914.
5th Norfolk Regiment.
Served in Mediterranean Expeditionary Force at the Dardanelles, viz., Suvla Bay.

SNOW, William, Junr., Signaller.
Gardener (Barton Manor).
Joined 6th November, 1915.
87th Siege Battery, Royal Garrison Artillery.
Arras, April-May, 1917; Cambrai, November, 1917; Arras, August, 1918; Cambrai, September, 1918.

SOANES, William James, Private.
Team-man, Farm, Sandringham.
Joined, 19th June, 1916.
9th King's Own Royal Lancasters.
Salonica.

SPRAGGE, Basil Edward, Lieut.-Colonel, D.S.O.
Gentlemen-at-Arms.
2nd Loyal Suffolk Hussars.
Raised and Commanded the 2nd Loyal Suffolk Hussars, 1914-16.
Headquarters, 4th Corps, British Expeditionary Force, 1917-18; graded as D.A.Q.M.G.
Battle on Cambrai Front, 21st-30th November, 1917.
Buying Horses for Government Remounts, August, 1914.
Special Constable, Suffolk County; now Assistant Country Director, Red Cross, Dumfrieshire.
Mentioned in Despatches.

STEEL, Ernest, Staff-Sergeant.
Gardens, Sandringham.
Joined, August 4th, 1914.
Corporal, Sergeant, Staff-Sergeant.
1st 5th Norfolks, Territorials; Royal Engineers.
Gallipoli; Pigeon Expert under War Office.

STEWART, William.
Windsor Royal Gardens.
Joined, 23rd November, 1914.
Oxford and Bucks Light Infantry; 2nd Hampshire Regiment; East Kent's; 22nd Royal Fusiliers.
Dardanelles, 1915. France, 1917—Ypres, Boulogne Wood, etc.
Invalided from Dardanelles and France.

STOCKWELL, Albert Edward, Bombardier.
Royal Mews.
Joined, 5th August, 1914.
Royal Horse Artillery.
Bombardier.
Mons, Cologne.
Military Medal.

SYKES, Reuben, Albert, Private.
Gardens, Sandringham.
Joined, 3rd April, 1915.
Royal Army Medical Corps.
Somme, Hamel, Messines, Coast Battles, Mont St. Quentin, Passchendaele, Ypres. Continued fighting from Villers Bretonneux, Hindenburg Line to Avesnes.

TAYLOR, Frank, Private.
Windsor Royal Gardens.
Joined, December, 1915.
Royal Berks Regiment.
Somme and Peronne.

TAYLOR, Oswald James, Temporary Major.
Gatekeeper, Windsor.
Joined, Royal Marines, 1914.
Sub-Lieutenant, Royal Naval Volunteer Reserve. Royal Marines; Attached Royal Army Ordinance Department.
September, 1914, Dunkirk and Antwerp; March, 1915, Egypt, Suez Canal; April, 1915, to January, 1916, Gallipoli; January, 1916, Mudros; April, 1916, Salonika; May, 1916, to May, 1919, France.
Staff Officer, Royal Naval Division, 1914 to 1916.
Twice mentioned in Despatches.

TOMPKINS, Arthur, Corporal.
House Porter, Lord Chamberlain's Department.
Corporal.
Grenadier Guards and Household Batt.
France—Somme, Arras, Ypres, Cambrai, Mandeberg; Army of Occupation, Germany

(C) SERVED IN A THEATRE OF WAR OR AFLOAT

TURK, Frederick Thomas, Sapper.
Waterman, Lord Chamberlain's Department.
Joined, 11th December, 1915.
Inland Water Transport, Royal Engineers.
France, 30th April, 1917, to 1st February, 1919. Volunteers, August, 1914, to March, 1917. Built Red Cross Launch for Red Cross Society for Service in Mesopotamia; Boat No. 950.

TWYNAM, Alfred.
Steward's Room Assistant, Lord Steward's Department.
13th London Regiment (Kensington Rifles).
France and Belgium.

VILLIERS, Charles Hyde, Lieut.-Colonel.
Gentlemen-at-Arms.
City of London Yeomanry, s.s. *Scotian*; Suffolk Yeomanry; Norfolk Yeomanry; Warren Heath Camp, Ipswich.
Lieut.-Colonel Commanding the 1 1st City of London Yeomanry on s.s. *Scotian* to Cape Helles, Gallipoli, then Ismailia and Suez and Suez Canal, Mediterranean Expeditionary Force.
" Mentioned."
Invalided with dysentry from Suez Canal.

VYSE, Charles Arthur, First Class Petty Officer.
Royal Mews.
Joined, August, 1915.
H.M. Balloon Ship, *Manica*; H.M. Sloop, *Cyclamen*; H.M. Sloop, *Honeysuckle*; H.M. Sloop, *Berberis*; H.M. Sloop, *Veronica*.
First Class Petty Officer; Observer.
German East Africa, January, 1916. Battle of Salita Hill, June, 1917. Adriatic Sea, August, 1917, to February, 1919.

WALDEN, Samuel George, Lance-Bombardier.
Gamekeeper, Castle Rising Shooting, Sandringham.
Joined, 7th June, 1916.
Lance-Bombardier.
Royal Garrison Artillery.
Somme, Nieuport, Arras.

WALKER, Frederick William, Lance-Corporal.
Woods, Sandringham.
Joined, 14th May, 1918.
Lance-Corporal.
H.M. Transport, *Abuvais*, No. 817.
4th Norfolks; 3rd Norfolks.
Deningham Platoon, Volunteers, Private No. 543, 3rd Naval Volunteer Reserve.

WALKER, Thomas, Sergeant.
Royal Mews.
Joined, 7th August, 1914.
Royal Engineers.
Private to Acting - Company - Quartermaster - Sergeant and Company-Sergeant-Major.
Despatch Rider throughout Retreat from Mons, Battle of Cateau, Battle of the Marne, Advance from Marne to Aisne, Battle of Ypres, Loos, Battle of the Somme; Ypres, 1917; Retreat from Somme to Villers-Bretoneaux, 1918; Offensive leading up to the Capture of Lille.
Military Medal, Royal Victorian Medal.

WALTON, Alfred Ernest, Private.
Milk Boy, Farm, Sandringham.
Joined, 28th May, 1915.
3rd Norfolks; 8th Norfolks; 2 7th Essex; 4th Reserve Essex; 5th Section, 58th Batt., Machine Gun Corps.
Two big operations, one in July, 1916, one in August, 1918; Several minor engagements.

WARD, Major the Honourable Sir John Hubert, K.C.V.O.
Equerry.
Military King's Messenger.
From Captain to Major.
Twice mentioned in Despatches.

WARD, William Dudley, M.P., Lieut.-Commander, Royal Naval Volunteer Reserve.
Vice-Chamberlain.
Joined, October, 1914.
Auxiliary Patrol.
Patrolling South-West Ireland, 1914-15.
Examination Service Dover Patrol, 1915-17.

(C) SERVED IN A THEATRE OF WAR OR AFLOAT

WATSON, Colonel Sir Harry Davis.
Equerry (Extra).
G.O.C., 32nd Indian Infantry Brigade, October, 1914, to January, 1916.
G.O.C., 20th Indian Infantry Brigade, January, 1916, to 6th January, 1918.
G.O.C., Northern Canal Section, 19th November, 1916, to 2nd May, 1917.
G.O.C., Palestine Line of Communication Defences 3rd May, 1917, to 31st August, 1917.
G.O.C., Composite Force, 1st September, 1917, to 14th November, 1917.
G.O.C., Force in Egypt, 7th January, 1918, to 26th March, 1919.
G.O.C., Cairo District, 27th March, 1919, to 31st July, 1919.
Chief Administrator, O.E.T.A. (South), 1st August, 1919, to 31st December, 1919.
Action in Suez Canal, February, 1915.
Third Battle of Gaza, November, 1917.
Temporary Major-General, 7th January, 1918, to 31st December, 1919.
K.B.E., C.B., C.M.G.; (Order of Nile, 3rd Class; Officier Legion d'Honneur; Commander St. Maurice and St. Lazarus; Commander Crown of Italy).

WATTS, William, Private.
Under Gamekeeper, Sandringham.
Joined, 1st September, 1914.
1 5th Norfolks.
Gallipoli, Suvla Bay.

WEBB, Harry.
Windsor Royal Gardens.
Joined, October, 1916.
Boy, 1st Class; Able Seaman.
Navy—H.M.S. *Thunderer*.
Able Seaman, Grand Fleet.

WELLING, Alfred William, Gunner.
Windsor Royal Gardens.
Joined, 15th December, 1916.
Royal Garrison Artillery.
France and Belgium—Hill 70, Lens, Arras, Nieuport, Dixmude, Menin, Dickybush.

WELLS, Frederick, Acting Sergeant
Engineers' Department, Sandringham.
Joined, 1914 and 1915.
Lance-Corporal, 2nd Corporal, Corporal, Acting/Sergeant.
5th Norfolk Territorials, 1914; Royal Engineers, 1915.
France with 34th Division.

WEMYSS, Rosslyn Erskine, Lord Wester Wemyss of Wemyss, Admiral of the Fleet.
Extra Equerry.
Vice-Admiral, Admiral, Admiral of the Fleet, K.C.B., G.C.B.
Commanding Cruiser Force, 9th August, 1914, to February, 1915.
Rear-Admiral in Mediterranean during Gallipoli Campaign, February, 1915, to December, 1915.
Landing at Helles on 25th April, 1915.
Evacuation of Suvla and Anzac, December, 1915.
Commander-in-Chief, East Indies, January, 1916, to July, 1917.
Deputy First Sea Lord, August, 1917, to December, 1917; First Sea Lord, December, 1917, to November, 1919.
Grand Cross, Legion of Honour.

WEST, Sidney, Driver.
Royal Mews.
Joined, 7th September, 1914.
Royal Field Artillery.
Western Front, 1915-19.

WHINCUP, J., Driver.
Royal Mews.
Joined, 21st February, 1916.
Royal Horse Artillery.
Somme, Loos, Lens, Ypres, Perone, Cambrai, St. Quentin.

WHITELAND, William, Corporal.
Windsor Royal Gardens.
Joined, 16th January, 1915.
Gunner to Bombardier, Bombardier to Corporal.
Royal Field Artillery.
France and Belgium—Loos, Ypres, Vimy Ridge, Somme, Messines Ridge, Passchendaele Ridge, Amiens.

(C) SERVED IN A THEATRE OF WAR OR AFLOAT

WILES, R., Driver.
Royal Mews.
Joined, 8th September, 1914.
Royal Field Artillery.
France, 1914 to 1917.

WILLANS, Frederic Jeune, Lieutenant.
Assistant-Doctor at Sandringham (Sir A. Manby's Assistant).
Joined, 1st June, 1917.
10th Field Ambulance, 1st Batt., Royal Warwickshire Regiment.
Passchendaele, 1917.

WINCHESTER, Frederick, Private.
Royal Mews.
Joined, 17th October, 1914.
Royal Berkshire Regiment.
Somme; Ypres; Asiago, Piave.

WOODHOUSE, Frederick, Lance-Corporal.
Gardener, Appleton Gardens, Sandringham.
Lance-Corporal.
1 5th Norfolks; (I.W.T.) Royal Engineers.
Suvla Bay. Egypt. Mesopotamia. Storeman (I.W.T.), Royal Engineers.
Trench feet, Malaria, Dysentry.

WOODWARD, Frederick Henry, Sergeant.
Sandringham.
Joined, 10th November, 1911. Mobilised 4th August, 1914.
5th Batt., Norfolks.
Sergeant.
Gallipoli, Suvla Bay, Anafarta. Egypt and Palestine. Battle of Gaza and El Terek.

WRAY (John) Cecil, Brigadier-General.
Yeoman of the Guard.
Temporary Brigadier-General, August, 1914.
Canadian Royal Artillery—47th Division, 57th Division, 64th Division.
Festubert, May, 1915; Loos, September, 1915; Commanded Eight Batteries of French Artillery, June and July, 1915; Passchendaele, 1917; Lys, 1918.
C.B., C.M.G.; four times mentioned in Despatches; Brevet of Lieut.-Colonel in Reserve of Officers.

WYLDE, Frederick, Battery Sergeant-Major.
Royal Mews.
Joined, 5th August, 1914.
Royal Horse Artillery, 1st Cavalry Division.
Battery Sergeant-Major.
Retreat of Mons, 1914; Loos; Bully Grenay, Vermelles; Givenchy; Ypres; Lievin (Vimy) Fleur Baix; Festubert; Richbough; St. Vasst; Bois Grenay; Foss.
Meritorious Service Medal.

WYNESS, George, Driver.
Farm Labourer, Invergelder.
Joined, 9th September, 1914.
Army Service Corps, Horse Transport, 8th Divisional Train.
France—6th November, 1914 to 17th February, 1919.

YALLOP, Albert, Ordinary Seaman.
Gardens, Sandringham.
Joined, 14th January, 1917.
H.M.S. *Suffolk*.
Siberian Expeditionary Force; Seaman on board H.M.S. *Suffolk*, and Guard Duties Ashore, Vladivostock.

(D) SERVED AT HOME

ALDERMAN, Mark, Private.
Windsor Royal Gardens.
Joined, April, 1916.
Royal Army Service Corps.
Home Service.

AMOS, Alfred, Sergeant.
Gamekeeper, Sandringham.
Corporal, Sergeant.
1/5th Norfolks, at home; 2/5th Norfolks, at home; 11th Norfolks Labour Corps, at home.

APPLETON, James William Sallis, 2nd Lieutenant.
Clerk to the Deputy-Ranger.
Joined, 3rd January, 1916.
2nd Lieut., October, 1918.
Royal Air Force.
England.

ASKER, William Howard, Private.
Work in Pheasantries, Sandringham.
Joined, 22nd November, 1915.
5th Norfolks, Labour Batt.
Served 12 months on the East Coast; two years in Agricultural Labour Corps.

BARLOW, Thomas, Private.
Labourer, Farm, Sandringham.
Joined, 9th March, 1916.
Labour Corps, at home.

BARNARD, William, Trooper.
Marshalman, Lord Steward's Department.
Joined, 17th November, 1914.
Royal Horse Guards.

BARNES, Henry.
Windsor Royal Gardens.
Joined, December, 1917.
Devons, Labour Batt.
Home

BATTERBEE, G. T., Private.
Farm Labourer, Sandringham.
Joined, 17th September, 1918.
4th Reserve Batt., The Buffs.

BELLEW, Lawrence, Regimental-Sergeant-Major, D.C.M.
Yeoman of the Guard.
Joined 28th December, 1914.
Regimental-Sergeant-Major, Lieutenant, Captain.
Duke of Wellington's Regiment; Lieutenant, West Yorkshire Regiment; Commandant of Four Prisoners of War Camps.

BENFIELD, Sydney, Sergeant.
Windsor Royal Gardens.
Joined, September, 1914.
Royal Berks.
Home Service.

BLAKE, Henry, Private.
Boy in Gardens, Balmoral.
Joined, 9th February, 1918.
Air Force Training and Machine Gun Corps.
Home Service.

BLAND, Albert Daniel, Cadet Pilot.
Technical School, Sandringham.
Joined, 22nd May, 1918.
Cadet Pilot.
Royal Air Force, Home Service Squadrons.

BLYFIELD, Arthur Vincent, Private.
Footman.
Joined, 3rd September, 1914.
8th Norfolk Regiment.

BOWMAN, Alfred Lewis, Private
Estate Carpenter, Sandringham.
Joined, 10th June, 1916.
Norfolks, 2 5th Yorks, Royal Engineers.
Forth Defences, Royal Engineer Services.

BREMNER, John, 2nd Lieutenant.
Estate Clerk of Works at Balmoral.
Joined, 5th April, 1918.
Air Construction Service, Royal Air Force.

BRIDGES, Albert George, Aircraftsman, 1st Class.
Carpenter, Sandringham.
Joined, 21st June, 1917, Royal Naval Division; 1st October, 1917, Royal Air Force.
Aircraftsman, 2nd Class to 1st Class.
5th Norfolks; 63rd Reserve Royal Naval Division; Royal Air Force.
Southern Area and North-Eastern Area, England.

(D) SERVED AT HOME

BRIDGES, Arthur, Private.
Sandringham.
Joined, 1914.
1 5th Norfolk Regiment.
Died in Lynn Hospital, 13th March, 1915.

BRIDGES, Frederick Thomas John, Private.
Gamekeeper, Sandringham.
Joined, December, 1915.
64th Provisional Batt., Suffolk Regiment; Royal Defence Corps.
Special Constable from formation till joining His Majesty's Forces; Officer's Servant till demobilised.

BROOMHALL, F.
Windsor Royal Gardens.
Joined, 2nd August, 1918.
Royal Warwicks.
Ireland.

BROWN, Frederick, Private.
Sandringham.
Joined, 4th May, 1918.
11th Bedfords; 19th Queens; R.A.S.C. (M.T.).

BUNN, James William, Private.
Carpenter, Sandringham.
Joined, 14th September, 1916.
2 5th Princess of Wales' Own Yorkshire Regiment.
Army Reserve Munition Worker, 1917; Pulham Admiralty Air Station; Harwich Submarine Depôt for Admiralty; Narborough Aerodrome for Air Ministry on construction work.

CAMPBELL, Charles, Lieut.-Colonel, C.I.E.
Gentleman-at-Arms, Lord Chamberlain's Department.
Joined, 12th November, 1914.
Royal Defence Corps, T.F.; Royal Air Force.
Section Commandant, No. 1 Lines of Communication, General Duties Unit, Royal Air Force.
Twice mentioned in Despatches.

CAMPBELL, Charles Smith, Private.
Plumber, Balmoral.
Joined, 13th June, 1916.
3rd Batt., Scots Guards.
Home Service.
Died of Pleurisy.

CAMPBELL, Edwin William, Squadron-Sergeant-Major.
Yeoman of the Guard.
Joined, 14th November, 1914.
Regimental-Sergeant-Major.
2 1st Duke of Lancaster's Own Yeomanry.

CARDRICK, Cyril.
Windsor Royal Gardens.
Joined, 7th December, 1916.
Royal Army Service Corps.
Home Service.

CEMERY, John Benjamin, Captain.
Yeoman of the Guard.
Joined, 25th July, 1915.
Captain and Quartermaster.
Royal Army Medical Corps,

CLAYTON, William, Private.
Sandringham.
Joined, December, 1916.
Essex Regiment.

COLES, James Harold, Private.
Royal Mews.
Joined, 25th July, 1915.
Royal Army Service Corps Remounts; 3rd Reserve Hussars.

COOK, Arthur, Private.
Windsor Farms.
Joined, September, 1914.
Royal Berks.

COOPER, James, Trooper.
Gamekeeper, Windsor. Deputy Rangers.
Joined, 30th July, 1918.
2nd Life Guards.
England.

(D) SERVED AT HOME

COPE, Henry, Quartermaster-Sergeant.
Yeoman of the Guard.
Joined, 28th January, 1915.
To Lieutenant.
Royal Army Ordnance Corps.
Lieutenant and Quartermaster in charge of No. 2 Company, Royal Army Ordnance Corps.

COTTERAL, G. W., Sergeant.
Royal Mews.
Joined, 10th September, 1914.
Dragoons, 2nd Berks Yeomanry.
Lance - Corporal, Corporal, Lance - Sergeant, Sergeant.

COX, William.
Windsor Royal Gardens.
Joined, December, 1916.
R.S.A.
Home Service.

CRICHTON, Honourable George, Colonel.
Assistant-Comptroller, Lord Chamberlain's Department.
Temporary Lieut.-Colonel, 17th July, 1915; Temporary Colonel, 7th February, 1917.
Coldstream Guards.
Adjutant, Reserve Batt., Coldstream Guards, 5th August, 1914, to December, 1914; Second in Command, Reserve Batt., Coldstream Guards, December, 1914, to 17th July, 1915; Commanding, Reserve Batt., Coldstream Guards, 17th July, 1915, to 7th February, 1917; Regimental Lieut.-Colonel, Coldstream Guards, 7th February, 1917, to 31st March, 1919.
Brevet-Lieut.-Colonel.

CRITCHETT, Sir Anderson.
Joined, 1916.
Surgeon-Oculist in Ordinary.
Senior Opthalmic Surgeon, King George's Hospital and The Acheson Hospital for Wounded Officers.

CUST, Captain Sir Charles Leopold, Bart., R.N.
Equerry.
Joined, October, 1915.
Admiralty.
Captain, Royal Navy.

DANIELS, Sidney, Private.
Gardens, Sandringham.
Joined, 10th June, 1916.
7th Suffolks.
Home Service.

DAVEY, Edward, Staff-Sergeant-Major.
Yeoman of the Guard.
Joined, 30th January, 1915.
Royal Army Service Corps.
Employed in Royal Army Service Corps, at Woolwich.

DAWSON, Sir Douglas Frederick Rawdon, Brigadier-General.
Comptroller, Lord Chamberlain's Department.
Brigadier-General for services in the War, 10th June, 1919.
War Office 18 months, and later General Head Quarters, Home Forces, Horse Guards.
A.D.P.S., War Office, 1914, 1915, during which he raised, organised and administered the Royal Defence Corps; Inspector of Vulnerable Points, General Head Quarters, Home Forces, 1916-17-18-19, with administration of Royal Defence Corps, and acting Adjutant-General for Volunteers to Commander-in-Chief, Home Forces.
C.B. (Military). Mentioned in Despatches.

DONALD, Duncan Alexander, Colour-Sergeant.
Yeoman of the Guard.
Joined, 2nd February, 1915.
Company-Quartermaster-Sergeant.
3rd Reserve Batt., Gordon Highlanders.
53rd Young Soldiers' Batt.

DORE, Sidney, Bandmaster.
Yeoman of the Guard.
Joined, 18th October, 1916.
Royal Defence Corps.

DOWDY, Arthur, Private.
Gardens, Sandringham.
Joined, 25th March, 1916.
Essex Regiment.

(D) SERVED AT HOME

DUGDALE, Frank, Lieut.-Colonel, C.V.O,
Queen's Household.
Warwickshire Yeomanry.
First line, 4th August, 1914, to October, 1914; Second line, October, 1914 to January, 1916; Transferred to Territorial Force Reserve.

DUGUID, Charles, Private.
Woods Labourer, Birkhall, Balmoral.
Joined, 6th September, 1914; called up 20th July, 1916.
7th Gordon Highlanders, Highland Cyclist Batt., Labour Corps, 3rd Gordon Highlanders.
Agricultural Company.

DUGUID, George, Private.
Gardener's Labourer, Birkhall, Balmoral.
Joined, 9th February, 1917.
Army Reserve Munition Worker.

DUNGER, George, Sapper.
Sandringham.
Joined, 31st March, 1915.
Royal Engineers.

EDWARDS, F., Trooper.
Royal Mews.
Joined, 11th December, 1914.
2nd King Edward's Horse.
Died in Hospital (consumption), 5th November, 1916.

ELIOT, Montague Charles.
Gentleman Usher, Lord Chamberlain's Department.
Joined, 28th November, 1914.
Lieut.-Commander, September, 1916.
Royal Naval Volunteer Reserve, H.M.S. *President* and H.M.S. *Impregnable*.
Naval Intelligence Division; Served on Staffs of Admiral Sir George Egerton, Vice-Admiral Sir George Warrender, Admiral Sir Alexander Bethell, and Vice-Admiral Sir Cecil Thursby, Commanders-in-Chief, Devonport, as Naval Intelligence Officer, from 28th November, 1914, to 20th February, 1919; August to September, 1914, Secretary, Q.M.N.G., St. James's Palace; September to November, 1914, Assistant-Commander, "C" Division, Metropolitan Police Special Constabulary.

EMERY, George, Petty Officer.
Boatman, Virginia Water. Deputy Rangers.
Joined, 2nd August, 1914.
Chief Petty Officer, 1917.
Victory (Portsmouth), *The President*, *Victory VI*.
England.

FASEY, John Henry, Private.
Gamekeeper, Windsor. Deputy Rangers.
Joined, 24th July, 1918.
Royal Army Service Corps.
England.

FEGAN, Daniel, Sergeant.
Yeoman of the Guard.
Joined, 14th August, 1914.
Quartermaster-Sergeant.
King Edward's Horse Yeomanry.

FELLOWS, Alfred Henry, Lance-Corporal.
Assistant Metal Smith, Windsor Castle, Lord Chamberlain's Department.
Joined, 10th December, 1915.
Lance-Corporal, May, 1917.
Royal Army Medical Corps.
Duty at War Hospital, Dartford, Kent.

FIRTH, Albert Lyas Bishop, Sapper.
Carpenter's Department, Sandringham.
Joined, 9th December, 1915.
2nd Provisional Company, Royal Engineers; Royal Flying Corps; 2 6th Norfolks; I.W.T., Royal Engineers.
March Offensive, 1918. First Army Area. Coastal Patrol Wireless and War Signal Guard attached to Admiralty. Royal Flying Corps—employed on Aerodromes at Farnborough. I.W.T., Royal Engineers—transportation of mechanical stores, etc.

FITT, Albert Henry, Sergeant.
Gardens, Sandringham.
Joined, 4th August, 1914.
Lance-Corporal, Corporal, Sergeant.
1 5th Norfolks, Army Cyclist Corps, 4th Lincolns.
Physical Training and Bayonet Fighting Instructor.

(D) SERVED AT HOME

FITT, William Joseph, Aircraftsman, 1st Class.
Golf Links, Sandringham.
Joined, 10th November, 1917.
Royal Air Force.

FLUDYER, Henry, Colonel, C.V.O.
Gentleman Usher, Lord Chamberlain's Department.
Scots Guards.
Commanding Scots Guards from August, 1914, to March, 1916.

FORD, Albert T., Private.
Engineers' Department, Sandringham.
1 5th Norfolks.
Home Service.

FORTESCUE, Captain Honourable Sir Seymour John, R.N., K.C.V.O., C.M.G.
Equerry.
Joined, August, 1914.
Admiralty.
Naval Censor, Press Bureau, under Admiralty.

FOSTER, William, Private.
Stud Groom, Sandringham.
Joined, 24th March, 1916.
Essex Regiment.
Discharged " unfit for service," July, 1916.

FRENCH, Houston, Captain.
Yeoman of the Guard.
Joined, 13th November, 1914.
Staff Officer under General Officer Commanding the London District.

FRIPP, Sir Alfred Downing, K.C.V.O., C.B., M.B., M.S., F.R.C.S.
Surgeon-in-Ordinary, Lord Chamberlain's Department.
Joined, 4th August, 1914.
Consulting Surgeon to the Hospital Ships, Royal Navy.
Had Hospital Yacht, *Sheelah*, as Headquarters in the Firth of Forth and Superintended the treatment of nearly all the wounded from the three North Sea engagements—Heligoland, Dogger Bank, Jutland.

FULCHER, Henry, Private.
Gardens, Sandringham.
Joined, 5th May, 1918.
London Rifle Brigade, 5th London Regiment.

GENT, Robert, Bombardier.
Windsor Royal Gardens.
Joined, 6th April, 1916.
Gunner to Bombardier.
Royal Garrison Artillery.
Home Service, Coast Defence Irish Command.

GOODING, George, Major.
Clerk Comptroller, Lord Steward's Department.
From Captain to Major, 1919.
Coldstream Guards.
Quartermaster and Acting/Paymaster, Reserve Batt., Coldstream Guards.
Twice mentioned in Despatches.

GOODMAN, Leonard, Cadet.
Sandringham.
Joined, 2nd August, 1918.
Royal Air Force.

GORDON, Frank, Private.
Stalker, Balmoral.
Joined, 8th February, 1916.
Gordon Highlanders—Territorial Force and Agricultural Company.
Home Service.

GORE, St. John Corbet, Brevet-Colonel, C.B., C.B.E.
Gentleman-at-Arms.
Assistant Military Secretary, Aldershot Command.
C.B.E.

GOSS, George Hooks, Private.
Sandringham.
Joined, 25th April, 1918.
51st Batt., Royal Sussex Regiment.
Army of Occupation on the Rhine.

(D) SERVED AT HOME

GREENWOOD, Charles, Regimental-Sergeant-Major.
Yeoman of the Guard.
Joined, 9th January, 1915.
Cheshire Regiment.
Drill Instructor to Officers' School of Instruction.

GREVILLE, Honourable Alwyne, Lieut.-Colonel, C.V.O.
Equerry.
Essex Yeomanry.
C.V.O.
England and Ireland.

GROVE, Charles, Captain.
Second Messenger, Lord Chamberlain's Department.
Lieutenant and Adjutant, Prisoners of War Staff, 23rd October, 1915; Temporary Captain, 23rd August, 1917.
Coldstream Guards.
Rejoined 4th Batt., Coldstream Guards from pension, 18th August, 1914; Appointed Sergeant-Major, Prisoners of War Camp, Olympia, 18th August, 1914, to 19th December, 1914; Transferred to Stratford, London, E., with prisoners, 20th December, 1914, to 22nd October, 1915; Discharged free for the purpose of being appointed to a Commission, 23rd October, 1915; Gazetted Lieutenant and Adjutant, Prisoners of War Camp, Dorchester, 23rd October, 1915; Transferred to Jersey, C.I., 11th April, 1916; Transferred to Frongoch, North Wales, with prisoners, 16th February, 1917, to present date.
Mentioned in *London Gazette*, Field-Marshal Commander-in-Chief Home Forces, March, 1917.

HAIG, Lieut-.Colonel Arthur Balfour; Retired late Royal Engineers.
Equerry.
Royal Engineers.

HALL, Charles, Gunner.
Garden Boy, Balmoral.
Joined, 3rd April, 1916.
Royal Garrison Artillery.
Home Service.

HARDY, Herbert, Private.
Farm Labourer, Sandringham.
Joined, 30th May, 1916.
Labour Party, Royal Fusiliers.

HARLEY, C., Private.
Gamekeeper, Windsor. Deputy Rangers.
Joined, 25th October, 1916.
16th Essex Regiment.
England till June, 1917; Agricultural Company, June, 1917, to March, 1919.

HARLOW, Frank, Private.
Labourer, Sandringham.
Joined, 21st June, 1916.
4th Norfolks.

HATCH, John.
Windsor Royal Gardens.
Joined, 7th August, 1918.
Berks Yeomanry.
Ireland.

HATCH, Percy.
Windsor Royal Gardens.
Joined, February, 1917.
Royal Berks.
Ireland.

HATTEY, Charles.
Windsor Royal Gardens.
Joined, 30th August, 1914.
Royal Berks.
Home Service.

HAY, Hon. Arthur, Major.
Gentleman Usher, Lord Chamberlain's Department.
National Reserve, Surrey Volunteers, Royal Defence Corps.
8th Batt., Surrey Volunteers, February, 1916, to March, 1917; Captain, Royal Defence Corps, March, 1917, to January, 1919; Commanding Surrey National Reserve, March, 1915, to March, 1917.

(D) SERVED AT HOME

HERSCHELL, The Lord, Commander Royal Naval Volunteer Reserve.
Lord-in-Waiting.
Joined, November, 1914.
Intelligence Division, Admiralty.
Officier de la Légion d'Honneur.

HICKS, Robert, Trooper.
Windsor Farms.
Joined, October, 1916.
2nd Life Guards.

HOLT, Edwin Frederick, Troop-Corporal-Major, D.C.M.
Yeoman of the Guard.
Joined, 26th January, 1915.
To Lieutenant.
27th Supernumerary Company, Royal Warwickshire Regiment; Royal Defence Corps.

HOOKS, James.
Sandringham.
Joined, 8th March, 1917.
23rd Training Depôt Station.
Royal Air Force.

HOOKS, Stanley Edgar, Rifleman.
Assistant-Keeper, Sandringham.
Joined, 7th January, 1918.
11th Batt., Rifle Brigade.

HOUCHEN, Thomas, Private.
Engineers' Department, Sandringham.
Joined, 4th August, 1914.
1 5th Norfolks.

HOUCHEN, Thomas Henry, Aircraftsman, 2nd Class.
Gardens, Sandringham.
Joined, 1st January, 1918.
Royal Air Force.
One of Wolferton Sea Bank Patrol Scouts, first year of War.

HUBBARD, Charles E., Junior, Aircraftsman, 2nd Class.
Gardens, Sandringham.
Joined, 23rd August, 1918.
Southern Command, S.W. Area, Royal Air Force.
Store-Clerk in Royal Air Force, also aeroplane packer.

IRVINE, Charles Alexander Lindsay, Captain.
Gentleman Usher, Lord Chamberlain's Department.
General Staff Officer, 3rd Grade, War Office Department Chief Imperial General Staff, 5th August, 1914, to 15th November, 1918.

JONES, Ben, Private.
Windsor Farms.
Joined, February, 1915.
Army Service Corps.

JONES, Thomas, Private.
Gardens, Sandringham.
Joined, 12th November, 1915.
3rd Norfolks.
Volunteer as from April, 1917, 3rd Volunteer Batt., Norfolk Regiment.

KEY, Edward L., Lance-Sergeant.
Sandringham.
Joined, 19th April, 1918.
London Scottish, Gordon Highlanders.

LAVELL, Ernest, Private.
Windsor Farms.
Joined, April, 1915.
Army Veterinary Corps

LINES, Albert, Private.
Woodman, Sandringham Farm.
Joined, 5th August, 1914.
1 5th Norfolks, Royal Defence Corps, Royal Air Force.
Flare Party on night-landing ground under Air Ministry.

LINES, Sidney Aaron, Sergeant.
Engineers' Department, Sandringham.
Lance-Sergeant to Sergeant.
1/5th Norfolks.

(D) SERVED AT HOME

LIVINGS, George Henry, Private.
Coal Porter, Lord Steward's Department.
Joined, 7th October, 1914.
Lance-Corporal, Corporal.
4th Batt., Royal Berks Regiment; 21st Midland Batt., Rifle Brigade; Royal Defence Corps.

LLOYD, Wilford Neville, Colonel, C.B., M.V.O.
Honourable Corps of Gentlemen-at-Arms.
Commandant, Remount Depot, Ormskirk, September-October, 1914; Assistant-Quartermaster General, Southern Command, from January, 1915, to January, 1917; Assistant-Major-General of Administration, Eastern Command from March, 1917, to October, 1917.
Companion of the Bath, 1918.

LONGMUIRE, William, Colour-Sergeant.
Yeoman of the Guard.
Joined, 29th January, 1915.
Royal Lancaster Regiment.

LUCKING, Ernest Harry, Regimental-Sergeant-Major.
Royal Mews.
Joined, April, 1915.
10th Reserve Cavalry Regiment, No. 2 Cavalry Officers' Cadet School.
Regimental-Sergeant-Major, 1917.
Irish Command.
Mentioned in *Gazette*.

MACGILL, Campbell Gerald Hertslet, Major, M.V.O., T.D.
Assistant-Secretary, Board of Green Cloth, Lord Steward's Department.
Substantive Major, 1st June, 1916.
London Regiment (London Rifle Brigade).

MANN, George, Sapper.
Engineers' Department, Sandringham.
Joined, 8th August, 1914.
5th Norfolks (Territorials) and Royal Engineers (I.W.D.).
Belfast Shipyards, Gretna Munition Factory.

MAUNDER, Edwin James Soal, E.P. Officer, Privy Purse.
Naval Barracks, Portsmouth and Crystal Palace.
Naval Barracks, Portsmouth and Crystal Palace.

McGREGOR, James, Private.
Road Labourer, Balmoral.
Joined, 15th June, 1916.
4th Scottish Rifles, Gordon Highlanders' Labour Batt.
Home Service.

MELTON, Albert George, Private.
Horseman, Sandringham.
Joined, 9th May, 1916.
4th Norfolk Regiment, Labour Corps.

MEUX, Hon. Sir Hedworth, Admiral of the Fleet.
Extra Equerry.
Commander-in-Chief, Portsmouth.

MINNS, James, Private.
Sandringham.
Joined, December, 1913.
15th Norfolks, transferred to Labour Corps in England.

MORRIS, James, Colour-Sergeant.
Yeoman of the Guard.
Joined, 29th January, 1915.
14th Batt., Cheshire Regiment.

MORRISON, George.
Windsor Royal Gardens.
Joined, October, 1916.
Berkshire.
Home Defence.

MURRAY, Robert, Quartermaster-Sergeant, D.C.M.
Yeoman of the Guard.
Joined, 13th March, 1915.
Lieutenant and Quartermaster, Captain and Adjutant, Major.
15th Service Batt., Sherwood Foresters; 19th Reserve Batt., Sherwood Foresters; 3rd Garrison Batt., Northumberland Fusiliers.

(D) SERVED AT HOME

MUTLOW, Hector.
Windsor Royal Gardens.
Joined, October, 1918.
Royal Berks.
Home Service.

MYRTLE, Richard, Private.
Gamekeeper, Castle Rising, Sandringham.
Joined, 1st September, 1914.
5th Batt., Norfolk Regiment.

NEWELL, Richard, Private.
Windsor Royal Gardens.
Joined, 6th June, 1915.
4th Royal Berks, Reserve Defence Corps.
Home Service.

NEWLAND, George.
Windsor Royal Gardens.
Joined, 26th October, 1914.
Royal Berks.
Home Defence and Guarding Prisoners, etc.

NURSE, Ernest, Private.
Carpenter's Labourer, Sandringham.
Joined, 27th June, 1916.
3rd Batt., Queen's Royal West Surrey Regiment.

PAGET, Alwyn de Blaquiere Valentine, Colonel.
Gentlemen-at-Arms.
23rd Service Batt., Royal Fusiliers; 24th Service Batt., Royal Fusiliers.
Second in Command, 23rd Service Batt., Royal Fusiliers, 3rd November, 1914, to 19th November, 1914; In Command, 24th Service Batt., Royal Fusiliers, 20th November, 1914, to 18th June, 1915; Draft-Conducting Officer, 2nd September, 1916, to 23rd December, 1916; Special Constable, Surrey County, 1914 to 1918.

PAINTER, Walter Ernest, Corporal-Mechanic.
Queen Alexandra's Technical School of Woodwork, Sandringham.
Joined, 9th August, 1915.
1st Class Mechanic, Corporal-Mechanic.
Royal Naval Air Service.
Coastal Patrols in English Channel; Stationed at Dover Seaplanes and Dunkirk Seaplanes; truing-up, overhauling and re-building all classes of seaplanes, and going on test flights.

PARSONS, Harry, Sapper.
Stovesmith, Holyrood Palace, Lord Chamberlain's Department.
Joined, August, 1916.
Inland Waterways and Docks, Royal Engineers.
Fitter and Turner in machine shop at the "Mystery Port," of Richborough, Kent.

PERRINS, Thomas Henry, Private.
Drawing-room Attendant, Windsor Castle, Lord Chamberlain's Department.
Joined, 14th September, 1914
Royal Defence Corps (Royal Berks).
Garrison Duty, East Coast, and in Ireland.

PLEVIN, Henry, Lance-Corporal.
Gamekeeper, Castle Rising, Sandringham.
Joined, 11th December, 1915.
Lance-Corporal.
Norfolk Regiment.

PLUME, Ernest Edward, Private.
Gamekeeper, Castle Rising, Sandringham.
Joined, 7th June, 1916.
4th Essex Regiment.

POTTINGER, George, Sergeant.
Kitchen Porter, Lord Steward's Department.
Joined, 13th May, 1915.
Sergeant.
Middlesex Regiment.

PRICE, George, Sergeant-Major, D.C.M.
Marshalman, Lord Steward's Department.
Joined, 5th August, 1914.
Promoted to 1st Class Warrant Officer on re-enlistment.
Irish Guards.
Meritorious Service Medal and "Mention."

PRITCHARD, Isaac, Quartermaster-Sergeant.
Yeoman of the Guard.
Joined, 30th November, 1914.
To Regimental-Sergeant-Major.
Provost-Marshal's Department, London Command.

(D) SERVED AT HOME

RAMSDALE, William, Gunner.
Royal Mews.
Joined, 4th July, 1918.
Royal Garrison Artillery.

RAND, Charles, Bugler.
Sandringham.
Joined, 11th March, 1918.
4th Northampton Regiment
Home Service.

ROBERSON, John, Private.
Sandringham.
Joined, June, 1916.
3 1st Norfolk Yeomanry.

ROSS, Alexander McKenzie, Colour-Sergeant-Major.
Yeoman of the Guard.
Joined, 10th January, 1915.
Royal Garrison Artillery.

SCOTT, William Angel, Lieut.-Colonel.
His Majesty's Bodyguard.
Employed in Military Secretary's Branch, War Office, since 20th August, 1914, and still employed, 17th March, 1919.
Mentioned in Despatches, 14th March, 1918.

SCOUSE, J., Sergeant.
Royal Mews.
Joined, 10th September, 1914.
"D" Squadron, 2 1st Berks Yeomanry; 4th Cyclists' Brigade.
Died in Hospital, 12th October, 1918.

SHAFTESBURY, Anthony Ashley Cooper, Earl of.
H.M. The Queen's Household.
G.O.C., 1st South-West Mounted Brigade; G.O.C. Southern Mounted Brigade; G.O.C., 7th Cyclist Brigade; G.O.C., 3rd Cyclist Brigade.
Brigadier-General, 1914.
C.B.E. (Military Division).

SMITH, Percy, Private.
Sandringham.
Joined, 4th August, 1914.
1 5th Norfolks.

SPARKES, James, Sergeant-Major.
Yeoman of the Guard.
Joined, 17th July, 1915.
Lieutenant to Captain.
For General Service.
Employed as Adjutant, Prisoners of War Camp, Knockaloe, Isle of Man.

STANFIELD, John, Squadron Sergeant-Major.
Yeoman of the Guard.
Joined, December, 1914.
Served as Assistant Paymaster to the Oxford Territorial Force Association, December, 1914, to 31st May, 1919.

STILL, Arthur Horatio, Troop-Sergeant-Major.
Yeoman of the Guard.
Joined, 29th February, 1916.
West Kent Yeomanry.

STREATFEILD, Sir Henry, Colonel.
Extra Equerry.
Commanding Grenadier Guards.

TAYLOR, Charles, Trooper.
Road Labourer, Balmoral.
Joined, 5th August, 1914.
Scottish Horse Yeomanry.
Home Service.
Died—result of accident while on Military Service.

TAYLOR, W. L., Gunner.
Royal Mews.
Joined, 20th December, 1916.
Royal Horse Artillery.
Home Service.

(D) SERVED AT HOME

TIMS, Edwin, Colour-Sergeant.
Yeoman of the Guard.
Joined, 21st September, 1914.
Captain.
6th Hants Regiment, 17th Hants Regiment.
Commanding N.C.O. School, 227th Infantry Brigade.
M.B.E.

TINDAL, David, Private.
Windsor Royal Gardens.
R.H.C.
Home Service.

TITMAN, George Alfred, Private.
Clerk, Central Chancery of the Orders of Knighthood, Lord Chamberlain's Department.
Joined, 1st May, 1916.
21st (Reserve) Batt., The King's (Liverpool Regiment).
Served in Civil Staff of Anti-Submarine Division, Admiralty, 1917-19.
Invalided out September, 1916.

TREVES, Sir Frederick, Bart., Colonel, A.M.S.
Sergeant-Surgeon to the King, Lord Chamberlain's Department.
Army Medical Service.
President of the Headquarters, Medical Board at the War Office.

TRIBBLE, William James, Driver.
Royal Mews.
3rd July, 1918.
Royal Horse Artillery.

TRIGG, William.
Windsor Royal Gardens.
Joined 20th May, 1918.
Royal Field Artillery.
Home Service.

TULEY, Frank, Sergeant.
Gamekeeper, Castle Rising, Sandringham.
Joined, 1st September, 1914.
1/5th Norfolks.

WAITE, James Malcolm, Lieutenant.
Waterman, Lord Chamberlain's Department
Joined, 2nd November, 1914.
Corporal, 14th November, 1914; Sergeant, 18th December, 1914; Colour-Sergeant, 2nd January, 1915; 2nd Lieutenant, 11th February, 1917; Lieutenant, 11th August, 1918.
Middlesex Regiment, Worcestershire Regiment.
Training and Equipping Drafts; Duty on Coast Defence, Great Yarmouth; Garrison Cadet Batt. Attached 12th King's Own Royal Lancs. Regiment as Officer in Command Messing. Attached Department Controller-General Merchant Shipbuilding, Admiralty; Aeronautical Inspection Department, Ministry of Munitions; Inspection of Flying Boat Hulls; now in Command of all types of Experimental Hulls.

WAITE, Richard, Lance-Corporal.
Waterman, Lord Chamberlain's Department.
Joined, 13th October, 1914.
Lance-Corporal.
Queen's Westminster Rifles (16th London Regiment), 33rd Middlesex, Labour Corps.
Headquarters' Staff, Queen's Westminster Rifles, 38, Buckingham Gate, 1915, to January, 1916; Headquarters' Staff, No. 1 and No. 2 City of London Medical Boards, January, 1916 to 1918.
Honorary Testimonial of The Royal Humane Society on Vellum, for saving life in the Thames, 14th August, 1917.

WARNOCK, John James, Quartermaster-Sergeant.
Yeoman of the Guard.
Joined, 26th April, 1915.
3rd Buffs.
Clerk in the Royal Garrison Artillery Records.

WENTFORD, George, Private.
Farm and Estate hand, Wolferton Farm, Sandringham.
Joined, 22nd September, 1914.
National Reserve; 2 5th Norfolks; Royal Defence Corps; Royal Air Force—General Duty.
Home Service.

WHITMARSH, William Henry, Trooper.
Windsor Royal Gardens.
Joined, 4th January, 1918.
2nd Life Guards.

(D) SERVED AT HOME

WILLOUGHBY, Honourable Claude H. C., Brevet-Colonel.

Groom in Waiting in Ordinary to His Majesty, Lord Chamberlain's Department.

4th-14th, August, 1914, Horse Purchasing Officer, Nottinghamshire; 15th August, 1914, to 22nd May, 1915, Recruiting Officer, Worksop; November, 1914, Special Constable, Nottingham; 24th May, 1915, to 2nd July, 1915, Commanded Third Line, Nottinghamshire Yeomanry (Sherwood Rangers); 3rd July, 1915, to 30th April, 1916, Deputy Assistant-Director Remounts, Headquarters, Northern Command.

WOOD, Thomas, Sergeant-Major, D.C.M.

Yeoman of the Guard.

Joined, 23rd November, 1914.

Lieutenant.

2nd City of London Yeomanry.

WOODHOUSE, Percy, Cadet.

Gardens, Sandringham.

Joined, 2nd August, 1918.

Royal Air Force.

Training as Pilot; Volunteer, April, 1917 to August, 1918.

WOORE, Ernest Edward, Private.

Carpet Porter's Assistant, Windsor Castle, Lord Chamberlain's Department.

Joined, 16th January, 1918.

Labour Corps.

Working at Aerodrome Construction Camp, Chattis Hill, Stockbridge, Hants, and Royal Army Service Corps, Forage Department, "W" Compy., and Dining Hall Orderly at Labour Centre; previous to enrolment on duty for Air Raid alarms, St. John's Ambulance Brigade, Windsor and Eton Division.

YALLOP, George, Lieutenant and Adjutant.

Home Farm, Sandringham.

Joined, 1st September, 1914.

Enlisted 1914, and held every rank up to Lieutenant.

5th Batt., Norfolks; Royal Air Force.

Bombing Instructor and Physical Training Instructor, 25th Norfolks; Submarine Patrol Administrative Duties, Royal Air Force.

(E) VOLUNTEERS

ASH, Samuel.

Office Keeper, Lord Chamberlain's Department.

Joined, 15th February, 1917.

Lance-Corporal, 25th July, 1918.

2nd County of London Volunteer Regiment.

BARRY, Frederick William, Platoon Sergeant.

Senior Assistant, Royal Library, Windsor Castle, Lord Chamberlain's Department.

Joined, 30th April, 1917.

Acting Sergeant, June, 1918; Platoon Sergeant, September, 1918.

1st Volunteer Batt., Royal Berks Regiment.

BROWN, Ernest, Private.

Groom, Stud, Sandringham.

Joined, 28th December, 1917.

Training Reserve, Regiment 84.

Sandringham Volunteers, *i.e.*, 3rd Volunteer Batt., Norfolk Regiment, April, 1917 to December, 1917.

COOK, Thomas Henderson, Colour-Sergeant.

Head Gardener, Sandringham.

Joined, 4th August, 1914; Discharged, February, 1915; May, 1917, Territorial; 2nd Lieutenant, 3rd Volunteer Batt., Norfolk Regiment.

15th Norfolks.

(E) VOLUNTEERS

CROWE, Robert, Sergeant.
Shire Stud Groom, Farm, Sandringham.
1 5th Norfolk Regiment.
Discharged from 1 5th Norfolks, 12th May, 1915; Served as Sergeant in 3rd Volunteer Batt., Norfolk Regiment.

FIELD, George David.
Clerk to Paymaster of His Majesty's Household, Lord Steward's Department.
Joined, 1914.
Athletes Volunteer Force.

KEMP, Edward, Lance-Corporal.
Inventory Clerk and Photographer, Lord Chamberlain's Department, Windsor Castle.
Joined, August, 1914.
Lance-Corporal, 11th March, 1918.
Eton Volunteers, 3rd Batt., Oxon and Bucks Light Infantry.
Assisted the Military at Didcot and passed courses of Machine Gunnery.

LONGDEN, Clifford, Lieutenant.
Privy Purse Office.
Joined, April, 1915.
2nd County of London Volunteer Regiment.
Lieutenant, September, 1917.

OSGOOD, Frederic Stanley, Lance-Corporal.
Clerk, Lord Chamberlain's Department.
Joined, 12th June, 1917.
Lance-Corporal.
2nd Provisional Batt. (Westminster), County of London Regiment (Volunteers); Lewis Gun Anti-Aircraft Section.

PRIMROSE, Guy Rosebery, Sergeant.
Clerk, Estate Office, Sandringham.
1 5th Norfolks; Discharged, January, 1915; 2nd Lieutenant, 3rd Volunteer Batt., Norfolk Regiment, as from April, 1917.

STONOR, The Hon. Henry, Captain.
Deputy Master of the Household.
Joined, 1916.
Motor Transport Volunteers.

WILLIAMS, Richard Keen, Private.
Gamekeeper, Sandringham.
Joined, 9th December, 1915.
Suffolk Regiment.
Home Service; Sandringham Volunteers; Norfolk Special Constabulary.

WORLEDGE, Frederick John, Captain.
Accountant, Board of Green Cloth, Lord Steward's Department.
5th Volunteer Batt., Essex Regiment.

(F) SPECIAL CONSTABLES

GRANT, Arthur P.
Forester (Head Stalker), Balmoral.
Special Constable.

HYEM, Pearl Walter.
Junior Messenger, Board of Green Cloth, Lord Steward's Department.
Joined, 23rd March, 1915.
Joined the Special Constabulary, 23rd March, 1915

MACKINTOSH, Charles.
Stalker, Balmoral.
Special Constable.

McDOUGALL, William.
Upholsterer, Balmoral.
Special Constable.

RODDA, Horace Wyndham.
Under State Porter, Lord Steward's Department.
Joined 17th August, 1914, Special Constabulary.
Sergeant, March, 1915; Sub-Inspector, February, 1917; Inspector, September, 1918.
Long Service Badge.

SMITH, James.
Road Foreman, Balmoral.
Special Constable.

INDEX.

Categories—

A. Killed.

B. Wounded.

C. Served in a Theatre of War or Afloat.

Categories

D. Served at Home.

E. Volunteers.

F. Special Constables.

INDEX.

INDEX.

INDEX.

INDEX.

www.ingramcontent.com/pod-product-compliance
Ingram Content Group UK Ltd.
Pitfield, Milton Keynes, MK11 3LW, UK
UKHW051129260726
13967UKWH00010B/2939